THE IRANIANS
HOW THEY LIVE AND WORK

The Iranians

HOW THEY LIVE AND WORK

John Abbott

PRAEGER PUBLISHERS
HOLT, RINEHART & WINSTON

ISBN 0-03-042496-8

First published in the United States of America
by Praeger Publishers Division of
Holt, Rinehart and Winston
CBS Educational Publishing
A Division of CBS, Inc.

Printed in Great Britain

Contents

To my friends, both British and Iranian,
with whom I have had the privilege of
studying Iran.

TURKEY
U S S R
Khvoy
Jolfa
Marand
TABRIZ
Rezayeh
Lake Urmia
Mahabad
Zarrineh
Bijar
Mianeh
Maragheh
Ardabil
Rasht
Zanjan
Qazvin
Chalus
Babol
Bandar Shah
CASPIAN SEA
Semnan
TEHRAN
ELBURZ MOUNTAINS
HAMADAN
Karand
Kermanshah
Shahabad
Arak
Qum
Kashan
K
Dez
Dezful
Khersan
ZAGROS
R
ISFAHAN
Shahreza
MOUNTAINS
IRAQ
I
AHVAZ
Marun
Karun
Bandar Shahpur
Khorramshahr
ABADAN
KUWAIT
PERSIAN GULF
Bushehr
Firuzabad
Shiraz
Shul
Faza
Jahro
Mand
Kangan
SAUDI ARABIA
Land over 2000m (6560 ft)
Railways
0   50   100   150 miles
0   50   100   150   200   250 km

U S S R
Bojnurd
Neyshabur
MASHAD
Sabzevar
ud
Kashmar
I R
Tabas
N Birjand
AFGHANISTAN
Zabol
Zarand
Rafsanjan
Kerman
Zahedan
Khash
Saravan
Iranshah
PAKISTAN
Bandar Abbas
Jask
Chah
Bahar

Introduction

THE name 'Iran' is derived from the generic word 'Arya' used to describe the various tribes who moved out of Asia more than 3,000 years ago and who settled on the high plateau that separates the Caspian Sea from the Persian Gulf. 'Persia' was the name given to them by the Greeks but it was really a misnomer because it referred only to those people from Fars province in the southern Zagros Mountains. Reza Shah, father of the present Shah, decreed some fifty years ago that Iran should replace Persia as the national name embracing all peoples of the country. As Scots, Welsh and Irish have objected to the over-use of 'the English' as a descriptive term, so too have the Iranians to the word 'Persians'; but old habits die hard and now the present Shah has decreed that the words are interchangeable.

Iran means more than just a unified country. It is a conscious statement that the people are of Indo-European origin, and not Arab, and their civilisation pre-dates that of Islam and can be traced back to the vast empires of Darius and Xerxes. Their language, however, still remains known as Farsi.

To write about present day Iran is virtually impossible; the past, in whatever way it is interpreted, is real enough, the future may be speculated upon, but the present is subject to such change that it is impossible to capture. With an annual growth rate of 26 per cent in real terms, it is doubtful if any country of comparable size has ever developed so much in so short a time. What is of concern to an Iranian is not the present but what the nightmare of present activity will produce next year, or the year after, when he will have the opportunity of assessing what it means to be an oil-rich nation.

To understand Iran it is necessary to study three things: Iranian history, the Shah and oil—in that order. The lessons of history are notoriously difficult to unravel but some aspects of Iranian history are indisputable, not least the strategic importance of her geographic position. Russia has always had, and presumably always will have, interests in the Gulf coast as having the nearest and most approachable ports on the southern seas. As a land bridge between Europe and India, Iran's position has been of immense importance throughout history. The Great Powers have feared a powerful Iran and have frequently meddled in her internal affairs to prevent this occurring.

The Shah has studied his history and drawn his own conclusions. Coming to the throne in 1941 he has known near poverty and failure as well as unbelievable wealth and success. He must rate as one of the world's foremost rulers. His power is immense, his vision wide; not a decision is taken, one suspects, without his knowledge and certainly no position of authority is held without his approval. Puritan by nature, he expects as much from others as from himself. He is so closely involved with his country that the terms Shah and Government are virtually synonymous.

Much oil has flowed from Iranian oil wells already, but still more remains. At present, it is the country's greatest asset because it is what the world desperately needs, and is prepared to pay for. One day the world may not need it or Iran may not have it to sell—either way the effect on the country will be dramatic and that day will come within thirty years.

The Shah not only understands this but knows what must be done about it—at least as far as Iran is concerned. He has interpreted history in a particular way, he knows the strengths and shortcomings of his own people better than anyone, and he has a fair idea of what Iran needs in the future. He calls it 'The Great Civilisation'.

In preparing for this, Iran has become a prototype of a planned economy. The Fifth Plan currently dominates all aspects of Iranian life and seeks to apportion the enormous oil revenues in such a way as to achieve this utopia before the Shah retires, something which he hints at doing in the late 1980s.

There can be few countries as fascinating, exciting, tantalising or infuriating as Iran. To the historian, the patchwork of development over so long a period must be intriguing, to the tourist it remains a tantalisingly beautiful country, to the economist it is pure theory in action—to the politician a frightening enigma. To the majority, it remains an exciting place, where the people's self-confidence seems to override their naivety, and where frustrations eventually melt away when confronted by an age-old charm.

I

The Land

Iran is a country of physical and social contrast, a country leaping into the Westernisation of the late twentieth century while some of its peoples still migrate vast distances through the mountains twice a year as they have done for past millennia. It is a country of vast arid deserts of sand and salt, of lush green rain-forest, stark mountain ranges and the occasional glacier. Part of the country is below sea-level while Mt Damavand is the highest mountain between Europe and the Himalayas. The country must rank as one of the world's highest with the average height of the central plateau at over 1,000m.

The country is large—1·6 million sq km—almost as large as the nine countries of the Common Market, and a sixth of the size of the United States. Until recently it was a country with only a small population. In the early twentieth century the population was estimated to be 7·5 million; in 1976 it was 34·5 million. Once it was a country of farmers and nomads; now it contains cities as large, and diverse, as Tehran and Isfahan with 4·5 million and ·75 million people respectively.

South of the Caspian Sea and the Russian steppelands the Iranian plateau is the natural link between the East and Europe. The strategic importance of this part of the Near East, or Western Asia as the Shah declared it to be in 1974, has long been recognised. The British in India occupied some of the southern part of the country in the nineteenth century, while the Russians controlled the Caspian lowlands. World War II saw a further occupation by the same powers of similar areas.

The route from Russia to the Indian Ocean could well lie across this desert vastness.

A map of Iran resembles a slightly squashed square leaning towards the West. A land boundary with Russia exists for over 1,600km with other land boundaries separating Turkey, Iraq, Afghanistan and Pakistan. She has boundaries on two seas: 630km on the Caspian where she faces Russia, and 1,880km on the Persian Gulf where she faces Iraq, Kuwait, Saudi Arabia and the other Gulf States. Whereas most countries of the world have rivers draining from their heartlands to the sea, Iran is characterised by rivers flowing inland towards the great deserts, rivers which, in the main, evaporate before they even have the opportunity to form an inland sea.

On three sides of this great country, massive mountain ranges isolate the central plateau from the outside world and even on the remaining side, where the Pakistan/Afghanistan borders are to be found, are more hills and mountains, together with Iran's only active volcano, Mt Taftan. The traveller entering Iran by road from Europe on E23 will be stopped at the customs post at Bazargum. To his left he will see towering up from the fertile plateau Mt Ararat, with Little Ararat to its side, a classic volcanic-shaped mountain complete with ice-cap and glacier standing out incongruously in the summer heat. Mt Ararat is not actually in Iran but it seems almost to act as the focal point for the mountain geography of the country. Radiating out due east are the Elburz Mountains, to the south-east the mighty Zagros, to the north the Caucasus and to the west the hills of Anatolia.

The Zagros Mountains stretch from here in a wide sweeping arc down to Afghanistan. For several hundred kilometres they are a somewhat chaotic mass of rock but in Pusht-e-Kuh they form a dramatic mountain barrier towering over the Tigris-Euphrates plain. From Dezful onwards the mountains are never far from the Persian Gulf with only a narrow coastal littoral of scorched and wind-blown sands to separate them. Here is the geologist's perfect research area. Vast eroded anticlines of sandstone and limestone roll and pitch like a petrified monster of some bygone era. Toiling through a narrow gorge or climbing an exposed hillside, may not engender an affection for the land as the heat, and heat haze, make life almost insufferable. But from the air, early in the day before the heat haze has developed, what a view! No soil or vegetation, it seems, seeks to hide this massive tortured mass, a crumpled playground of the gods where rocks have been torn apart and pushed up and pulled down in a way almost disturbing to the human mind. Geologically, this area has been studied in more detail, perhaps, than any other section of the earth's crust. Here, in the early years of this century, geologists from the old Anglo-Persian Oil Company made an agreement with the Bakhtiari chiefs for the sole rights to prospect. Before the days of aerial surveying and seismic recorders, the geologists toiled through these mountain masses to build up a picture of the rock structure at depth: the faults, the domes, the salt-plugs, the permeable and impermeable stratas. From here oil first flowed in 1908. A refinery was built at Abadan which was to become the largest in the world. Now the crude oil flows in pipes a metre in diameter to the oil tanks on Kharg Island. On a clear morning the supertankers from Japan, Europe and America can be seen edging their way up to take on board another million barrels to keep the wheels of modern civilisation turning thousands of kilometres away. And, in exchange for Iran's black gold, the Japanese are building a vast petro-chemical plant on the coast at Bandar Abbas, the British a new steel complex at Isfahan and the French a metro system in Tehran.

Just how, why and when this vast earth movement occurred is one of the fascinating problems of modern geology. For long it was thought that all these rocks had been formed from deposits laid in one great geosynclinal basin. At some stage, it was surmised, the weight of the sediments caused the basin to sag, so buckling the sediments at the sides. But now new ideas are current. Plate techtonics was first conceived as a theory as recently as 1968 but it has revolutionised thought on the origins of land masses—not least in Iran. The land masses of the world are envisaged as being 'rafts' of granitic and sedimentary rock carried on constantly moving crustal material, or plates, formed by igneous material at their centres and, where they meet, being pushed back down into the earth where they again revert to a semi-liquid state. When two rafts are brought together at this convergence zone they are too light to sink and so get pushed further together, buckling, cracking and faulting as they do. Iran would appear to be right in the middle of such a zone with the Arabian plate edging towards the Asian, and receiving a further nudge from the Indian plate and its product, the Himalayas. For the traveller sceptical about such matters, let him first experience an earthquake in Shiraz or Tabriz, see the face of Kuh-e-Dinar, or the landslide at Kabir Kuh—and then just fly back along the Zagros ranges.

The Elburz range is narrower but contains a higher peak, Mt Damavand, at over 6,000m. Rising almost sheer from the Caspian coastal plain, itself only a kilometre or so wide in places, it is crossed by few passes, the main ones being at upwards of 3,300m. The long drive up these passes is hardly to be recommended for the nervous and those with a fear of heights. At the best of times Iranian driving has to be tolerated rather than believed; with buses vying with lorries, the smooth uninterrupted passage of a car on such roads is an impossibility.

The Elburz Mountain range is in many ways even more dramatic than the Zagros. Emerging out of the high and undulating hill country of Azerbaijan and the ancient country of the Armenians, the Elburz range parallels the southern shore of the Caspian, shutting it off from the desert heartland to the south. Towards the east, when already far past Gorgan and Shahrud, the range loses its altitude and angularity and, after the spectaclar peak of Mt Damavand, drops down to the rolling hill country of Kopet Dag on the Russian borders and the province of Khorasan around Mashad. On its north-facing slopes luxuriant vegetation is to be found. The hills are covered with scrub vegetation and forest up to an altitude of about 2,000m while much of the flat coastal plain has been cleared of its 'jungle' (the affectionate name used by Tehranis for the outback, similar to the attitude of the Londoner to Suffolk and Norfolk and the New Yorker to the valleys of Maine and Vermont). Here are fields of rice, cotton, tobacco and fruit, holiday villas and the caviar canning factory at Bandar Pahlavi.

It is a strange landscape. The Caspian is slowly evaporating, leaving the coastal plain to emerge as flat sandy land, every year getting steadily wider. The humidity is debilitating. On occasion the skies clear and the 'jungle', never far away, stands out a vivid olive green with the cold grey of the mountain peaks reaching still further above. But more often it is cloudy and the tourist is left to sweat it out quietly, while listening to the constant chatter of the crickets, or take refuge in a boat and make off shore! The people are staunchly independent and determined—the Scotland of Iran, it has been suggested. It even boasts a city, Rasht, whose inhabitants—so one is led to believe by the innumerable Rashti jokes in circulation—must be a curious mixture of Irish and Scots.

Great rivers flow from the mountains in spring, having cut for themselves deep gorges and deposited vast deltas of silt and gravel into the Caspian and so further extended the coastal plain. East of Bandar Shah, the railway terminus much used to take supplies to Russia during World War II, begins the Russian steppelands and beyond lies the desert of Kara Kum. This is an ancient landscape presided over by the great brick-built tower of Gombad-e-Kavus thought to date from AD 1006 but whose real origin and purpose seems to have been forgotten. Towering over this the great range of the Elburz continues to the east, merging with the Hindu Kush and the Himalayas.

A drive through the Elburz can be a highlight of a visit to Iran. Having survived the drive up from the Caspian along one of the five main mountain passes, the traveller takes a well needed rest at some tea-house (*chaikhaneh*) at the top. Away to the north the influence of the Caspian is still to be seen in the scrub vegetation but to the south, as the road makes its somewhat precarious way down to the central plateau, aridity is the dominant note to the landscape. The change is startling.

Within a few kilometres one has passed into the dry, vegetation-less, timeless heartland of Persia. Only in spring, when the snows melt, are the valleys filled with the turbulent mass of waters whose destiny is eventual evaporation or percolation in the deserts. But modern man's technology is fast changing this pattern. Great dams, such as that behind Qazvin or the one currently being built in the Lar valley (so destroying one of the most delightful country retreats from Tehran), are holding back these flood-waters for irrigation and hydro-electric purposes. The results are dramatic, leading as they do to increased agricultural output and expanding industry, not least as a spectacle with the establishment of a prestigious 'Yacht Club' some 50km from Tehran and at an altitude of 2,500m. No smarter speed-boats were ever seen in the Mediterranean than now speed across what were, until ten years ago, the summer pastures of nomadic tribesmen. Fears are expressed, however, about the effects of the weight of all the water in this earthquake-prone area and the inhabitants of Qazvin, who experienced an earthquake killing many thousands of people in 1964, remain sceptical as to its future. A more immediate problem is the silt which is carried off the exposed mountain slopes and threatens to fill completely the reservoir in less than a hundred years.

Water has long been the key to prosperity in Iran; in fact, even with the present dominance of oil, water and improved agriculture are still essential to the country's success. Persians developed a unique system of irrigation by the construction of *qanats*, long underground tunnels, to take water to otherwise arid and unproductive areas. These tunnels tap the water supply at the foot of the mountains where the water is held in the permeable sediments, often at depths greater than 150m. Some *qanat* systems are many kilometres in length. The tunnel is dug to give a slight dip towards the mountains. The digging and maintaining of *qanats* is a highly skilled job normally undertaken now by families from the Yazd area. Vertical shafts some 50m apart are dug along the line of the proposed tunnel and skilled *qanat* diggers dig the tunnel out in both directions from the base of each shaft. It is a very long and expensive process. The towns and cities of the central area depend almost entirely on *qanats* for their water supply and the countryside around appears pock-marked (especially when seen from the air) by the lines of the *qanat* holes. A complicated legal system regulates their control and maintenance.

The Central Basin covers some three-quarters of a million square kilometres, over half the total area of the country. While it is easy to refer to this in general terms as the Central Plateau of Iran and to generalise its altitude at 1,000m it is, obviously, a more complicated feature containing a number of separate basins, some as low as 300m, with ranges of low relief forming locally important features. During the wetter periods of the late Tertiary and early Quarternary it is thought that much of this area, like Afghanistan, was occupied by large inland seas. However, even then, it appears that the rainfall was never sufficient for any of these to overflow across the encircling ranges and so drain away to the sea. The aretic (internal radial) drainage continues to the present though the rainfall of less than 100mm per annum is obviously of little importance. In some of the basins salt lakes, *namaks*, are still to be found. Seasonally, these may sometimes support a shallow covering of water but normally they are dry and reflect the sunlight in a way which is almost blinding. Of somewhat similar form, and particularly Persian, are the *kavirs*. These are also areas of inland drainage fed by seasonal streams which supply quantities of fine silt sediments and salts in solution. The sediments are deposited and the salts precipitated out by evaporation, leaving a sticky and unstable slime. The salt forms the surface layers and gives the impression of a firm crust but the lower zone remains a highly viscous mud, frequently with channels of damper material which move through the *kavir*. Superficially, a *kavir* and a salt lake appear to be similar but the former is a dangerous and totally inhospitable place.

The Great Kavir, or Kavir-e-Bozorg, lies immediately to the south of the Elburz Mountains and extends for some 300km east and west. In reality it consists of several isolated basins but the whole area is virtually impenetrable with local tradition ascribing the missing legendary city of Lut, the Biblical Sodom, to the eastern section. It must remain doubtful if any settlement, let alone a city, could ever have existed in the Kavir. North of the Kavir, on the Elburz piedmont slope, are situated a number of settlements famous for many centuries as trading centres on the routes through to the Orient—the cities of Semnan, Damghan, Shahrud and Sabzawar. Controlling the land route with mountains behind and impenetrable *kavir* in front, these grew rich in the days of the caravan trade, but are now pale apologies of their former glory. The long distance Mercedes-Benz buses and lorries have replaced the camel and, being capable of travelling far greater distances each day, the caravanserai of today—the transport inn—are far fewer and further apart and certainly less glamorous than those of earlier days. The signs of human settlement along this belt are numerous: ruined castles, villages, mosques and endless *tells*— vast mounds standing up out of the desert masking settlements of an unknown age. Archaeologists have been busy here for many years and have so far made little impression on their vast numbers.

Most of the Central Basin, however, is made of firmer material than the Kavir. *Dasht* is the most common landscape, consisting of a mixture of rock fragments and silt well compacted and subject to little change in seasonal form. What precipitation there is tends only to consolidate the mass rather than to erode it. Sand is widespread but tends to be concentrated in the southeast, in the province of Sistan and in local patches around what would have been the shore lines of the early Quarternary inland 'seas'. In Sistan the sand formations are the result of strong local winds and a variety of dunes are to be found. Along the coasts of the Gulf, too, sand dunes mainly of the *barchan* type are frequent occurrences.

If the landscape of the Central Basin varies, the climate is similar across the whole area. As with the rest of the country, the highest temperatures are experienced in July and August with figures frequently over 40°C (104°F); winter conditions in the desert, while not as severe as those in the mountains, are nevertheless cold. The annual range of temperature for much of the Central Basin is in excess of 25°C (77°F). Snow falls heavily in the mountains and even Tehran, which in July has an average temperature of 29°C (84·2°F), has several months of snow, and ski-ing is a favourite winter sport on the slopes behind the city. The weight of snow lying on the airport roof at Mehrabad (Tehran) contributed to its collapse in December 1974. The majority of the Central Basin receives less than 100mm of precipitation per annum while the wettest part of the Caspian, that around Rasht, receives in excess of 1,800mm.

Climatically, Iran is a land of extremes. Even in midsummer the visitor who feels, on stepping out of his air-conditioned plane, that he is in an oven would do well to remember that a thin sweater will be needed in the evenings and a thick one if he is to travel the mountains. The dry, skin-cracking aridity of the deserts can be exchanged within less than a day's drive for the totally enervating humidity of the Caspian littoral.

2

The People

In 1971 Iran celebrated, with great pageantry, the 2,500th anniversary of the Monarchy. The main scene was set at Persepolis, a ruined palace of great dramatic form built by Darius, Xerxes and Artaxerxes in the fifth century BC and thought to have been sacked by Alexander the Great. The celebrations, which lasted for many months, culminated in a great spectacle set amidst the ruins showing the evolution of the Persian peoples in the two and a half millennia of history. Present were the heads of state from many countries and they were entertained in a vast luxuriant 'village' especially built amidst a grove of trees some distance from the old palace. Kings mingled with presidents in a splendour that few can previously have experienced and perhaps none were likely to see again. The Shah, Mohammed Reza Shah Pahlavi, entertained his guests amid this oriental splendour with the manner and the sophistication of Western Europe. The Shahanshah—King of Kings, Centre of the Universe, Shadow of the Almighty, Vice Regent of God—must have been the proudest of men that day when the whole panorama of Persian history unveiled itself before the eyes not only of his royal visitors but of the hundreds of millions of television viewers the world over. The confidence of the Shah, and the majority of his peoples, in what had been achieved was admirably demonstrated that afternoon. 'Old Persian hands' whose opinion of the people to organise even a minor operation was not high, were left amazed at the scale, the intricacy and the precision of this and other aspects of the celebrations. The scale and the efficiency of the armed services proved beyond all doubt that here was a country that had to be reckoned with, a power that was daily becoming stronger. Opposition to the celebrations, as well as opposition to the political system, certainly existed. Seen by some as the strength, and by others as the condemnation, of that system was the efficiency that prevented them from being apparent. But this should not detract unduly from the colossal achievement of which that day at Persepolis was the culmination or, seen almost from the point of history today, was a major milestone.

In 1921 Reza Khan, the Shah's father, had shared the leadership of a virtually bloodless coup and overthrown the weak government of the *Qajars*. Within two years of the coup he had become prime minister and in 1925 parliament deposed Ahmad Shah, the last of the *Qajars* and Reza Khan was crowned as his successor. The coup had not been difficult. The *Qajars* had been squandering their wealth and losing support for generations.

The Reza Shah had been born in 1878 in the Caspian province of Mazanderan. His family had military connections but were poor, his father dying when he was still an infant. At the age of fourteen he joined the Cossak Brigade and, by dint of private study and singlemindedness, gained a commission. He saw action in many campaigns 'especially against the rebellious tribes who were playing havoc with our towns and villages in many parts of the country'. At a later stage he fought some of the Bolshevik units. Not only did the influence of foreign powers within Persia sicken the young officer, so too did Persia's own internal difficulties, particularly the corrupt and inefficient administration of the *Qajars* and the almost independent and self-interested power of the tribes.

The end of the *Qajar* dynasty in 1925 did not immediately usher in better times. The Reza Shah was a man of formidable energy but the 1920s and 1930s were difficult times when the new dynasty could have easily been dislodged. At his accession the population of the entire country was little more than eight million and many of these owed but token allegiance to the Crown. In particular the tribes of the Zagros, especially those in Fars and Khuzistan, as well as Baluchistan, were fiercely independent. To understand Iran of today it is essential to understand two men: Persepolis saw many dynasties in its long history but the modern state is the work of the Reza Shah and his son, Mohammed Reza Pahlavi, who took the march past.

As an old soldier the Reza Shah knew the importance of good communication. When he was crowned the roads of Persia were so bad and so riddled with bandits that it was preferable to travel from Tehran to Mashad by way of the Caspian Sea rather than to attempt the road to the south of the Elburz. A special highway patrol was established and block houses built at strategic intervals to protect travellers on the major routes. Great energies went into the building of the Tehran–Abadan railway which took twelve years to complete from 1927; it was financed entirely by internal taxes as the Reza Shah feared any external financial commitment. Not only was he single-minded himself, he expected total commitment from all around him. The story is told of the time he was visiting a new section of the railway. Some hours before his arrival an engine fell off the rails. All means of raising it back on to the line failed and the men were in terror of what would happen when the Shah saw this. Shortly before his arrival a novel solution was found. Armed with spades, the men shovelled sand over the fallen engine and the Shah passed by later and noted nothing stranger than an unusual looking sand dune! A story perhaps typical of Iran but indicative of the attitude towards the Reza Shah. It is also told that, in an effort to improve the Civil Service he went to the Ministry of Finance just after opening time one morning, when many of the staff were not present, and ordered all the doors to be locked. A number of officials, including the Minister, arrived to find themselves shut out. Reza Shah had them all sacked!

If he expected much of others, Reza Shah gave unstintingly of himself. Although Shah, he continued to live the life of a simple soldier with considerable austerity, in marked contrast to the traditional opulence of an eastern monarch. Reforms went far further than roads, railways and the police to finance, education, military training and industrialisation. A full programme of Westernisation was commenced but, lacking the financial resources and the technical ability, this was initially a very slow process. With one eye over his shoulder watching the rapid progress being made by Turkey under Kamel Attaturk—with the advantages of greater contact with the West—and the other on his own land, Reza Shah saw all too clearly the problems ahead.

Reza Shah's rule was ended prematurely by the events of World War II. Although German influence in Iran had increased greatly during the 1930s, the Shah had frequently declared his country's neutrality. In June 1941 Germany invaded Russia and the Allies had to find rapidly a supply route to the Russian front. On 25 August 1941 British and Russian troops simultaneously invaded Iran from south and north on the pretext of preventing a German coup d'état. The invasion was completed within three days. On 16 September Reza Shah abdicated. He died three years later in Johannesburg. At the age of twenty-one Mohammed Reza Pahlavi succeeded his father as Shah. Asked in the early 1950s why he had not been crowned, the Shah immediately replied, 'I could not take pride in being crowned king of a nation such as we are today. But Iran will not stay like this. Our problems are big ones, but we have magnificent natural resources. And our greatest natural resource is the Persian people.' It was not until 1967 that the Shah crowned himself in a brilliant coronation ceremony in Tehran.

The year 1942 was a dark one for the Iranian people and for the young Shah. In January of the following year a Tripartite agreement was signed between Iran, Russia and the United Kingdom stating that all foreign troops would be removed from Persian soil within six months of the cessation of hostilities. In September 1943 Iran formally declared war on Germany.

The supply line to Russia was operated by the British out of Bandar Shahpur and Khorramshahr on the Persian Gulf to Tehran where the goods were taken over by the Russians. In late 1942 the American Persian Gulf Service Command added a further 30,000 men to the Allies' operations. Extra railway engines were imported, railways and roads were improved and the total capacity of the transport system had increased tenfold by May 1943. Many are the stories still recounted by the Allied ex-servicemen of conditions at the ports: unloading ships in temperatures of 60°C (140°F), blinding snow storms in the Zagros, indescribable road conditions. Over five million tons of war supplies were moved. The Iranian economy was not able to stand the strain of the occupation and the accompanying inflation. The Middle East Supply Centre was established by the British and Americans to give both material and technical advice to the Persians. In November 1943 Churchill, Roosevelt and Stalin attend the Tehran Conference. The Declaration of that December included the following:

> *The Governments of the U.S.A., U.S.S.R. and the U.K., are at one with the Government of Iran in their desire for the maintenance of the independence, sovereignty and territorial integrity of Iran. They count upon the participation of Iran, together with all other peace-loving nations, in the establishment of international peace, security and prosperity after the war, in accordance with the principles of the Atlantic Charter, to which all four Governments have continued to subscribe.*

If this gave grounds for optimism it was premature. Iran had still more difficult times to pass through before Persepolis could be reached. Even though the US, USSR and UK had agreed that their troops would withdraw from Iran within six months of the ending of hostilities, this did not happen. The Russians had supported the formation of the Autonomous Republic of Azerbaijan in August 1945 and considerable diplomatic efforts were required to remove them, including the lodging of the first complaint before the UNA.

The years immediately following the war were ones of extreme financial stringency. Eventually, in 1950, some aid was granted by the US under its Point Four Programme and the first of the Seven Year Development Programmes was implemented. The money available was far too small—a loan of $25 million—and anti-American feeling ran high. Negotiations with the Anglo-Iranian Oil Company for increased royalty payments dragged on and appeared to get nowhere, while eventually a $20 million trade agreement with the USSR was signed to stave off immediate economic collapse. In March 1951 the Oil Company was nationalised and shortly after ceased its operations.

Dr Mossadegh, an elder statesman of extreme xenophobic tendencies, rose to power. Mossadegh showed extraordinary ineptitude in handling negotiations, repudiated the Stokes Mission which offered an equal sharing of the oil revenues and, when the British Government referred the matter to the International Court at The Hague on the basis of the 1933 agreement with Reza Shah, refused to recognise the Court's jurisdiction. In July 1952 the Shah granted Mossadegh extraordinary powers to govern without recourse to Parliament for six months. The International Court stated that it had no jurisdiction in the oil dispute and the situation deteriorated still further. Mossadegh rejected all appeals made to him by Truman, Eisenhower and Churchill; the National Assembly (*Majlis*) was denuded of most its powers and the mob became more powerful. Martial law was extended, extra paper money circulated and inflation increased. The Supreme Court was dissolved and election to the National Assembly suspended. The Press was stifled. In June 1953 Eisenhower threatened to limit American aid. By August opinion turned dramatically against Mossadegh and the Shah was able to dismiss him. Trials followed later and the pro-Communist Tudeh party which Mossadegh had allowed to prosper, particularly in the Army, was ousted. Zahedi took over as Prime Minister and Eisenhower authorised an immediate payment of $45 million of economic aid to make good the deficit in the revenue. Negotiations were immediately started for the establishment of an International Oil Consortium to replace the Anglo-Iranian Oil Company but it was a further year, October 1954, before oil began to flow again. The date 19 August (28 Mordad in the Iranian calendar), the day Mossadegh was overthrown, is still kept as a national holiday.

Mossadegh did, however, perform one valuable service for his country: he allowed the full extremes of nationalism that had been fed by the economic and political crises of previous years to erupt. Behind the wild adulation with which this man, so frequently clad in his pyjamas, was greeted by the crowd was the pent-up fury generated by the capitulations, the war and economic disasters caused by—or at least blamed on—the foreigners. His rule saw a resurgence of nationalistic fervour which, as the oil remained in the ground and the country became progressively bankrupt, gave way to a far more realistic appreciation of international co-operation. It was an expensive, but necessary, lesson.

3

The People's History

As Mohammed Reza Shah Pahlavi took the salute at Persepolis that day in 1971 he, his country and the world were witnessing a great testimony to the achievement of a nation over a short span of years. To the Shah himself, and to his father, much of the credit for this progress must go.

When Persepolis was chosen for the site of the celebrations and the Shah made his visit to Pasargadae, to the tomb of Cyrus the Great, he was consciously linking his dynasty not only with a long and varied sequence of earlier dynasties which have all left their mark on the Persian people, but particularly to a time of pre-Islamic martial greatness. Was it at Persepolis that the Shah first dreamt of 'The Great Civilisation'—that state of materialistic utopia his people are now being led to expect at the end of the 1980s? Certainly the concept is not Islamic, nor is Islam Persian in the way in which Cyrus, Darius and Xerxes speak across the centuries of another period of Iranian greatness. The announcement of the new calendar in 1975 dating from the coronation of Cyrus 2,553 years before, would seem to reinforce the idea that the Shah's ambition is best understood in these historic, pre-Islamic, imperial terms.

The visitor to Persia would do well to remember as his first lesson that these people are not Arabs but of Aryan stock. It is thought that the Aryan peoples—hence its present official name of Iran—arrived in Persia about 1500 BC. As the Medes (who settled in the north-west of the country) and the Persians (who settled in the south) they figure largely in the Old Testament. At present some 68 per cent of the population speak Persian or some other Indo-European dialect. Farsi, the official name for the language, is taken from Fars province, that section of the Zagros Mountains inhabited by nomadic tribes folk. The Lurs and the Baluch, also nomads, speak a Persian dialect. More than a quarter of the population speak Turkic, although the only true Turkish stock are the Quashquai near Shiraz and the Turkoman on the north-east border of the country adjacent to Russia, a tribe renowned for its fine horses and distinctive geometric designed carpets. Minority groups, retaining their own language, religion and cultures are the Armenians, Jews, Arabs and Assyrians. None of these groups are really pure stock, however, and blood and language are well mixed. The kingdom ruled over by the Achaemedian dynasty, which was at its zenith during the reign of Darius and Xerxes about 500 BC, stretched from Greece and Libya in the west to the Indus in the east and across the Caucasus and to Chorasmia to the south of the Aral Sea. This was the first world empire of antiquity, vaster, more numerous in population and diverse in culture, than had been its predecessors Babylon, Egypt and Assyria. On the tomb of Darius was inscribed: 'I am Darius, the great King, King of Kings, King of the lands peopled by all races, for long King of this great earth, reaching even far away . . .'.

Mount Damavand. At over 6,000m this is the highest peak between Europe and the Himalaya; it completely dominates the Elburz mountain range. In ancient Zoroastrian belief, it was thought to be the bridge between earth and heaven. In winter, the lower slopes are popular with skiers

Isfahan. Few of the world's great cities make quite such an instant impact. The close juxtaposition of mountain, desert and the vivid green of the irrigated fields, combined with the tall delicate minarets, the blue domes of the mosques and the elegant archways and colonnades of the buildings, set against the brilliant blue of the sky, led to the claim that 'Isfahan is half the world'

A highly effective postal service was established by Darius which gave excellent internal communication and kept the Empire together. In particular, the royal road from Susa to Sardis in Asia Minor was an all-weather road with staging posts a day's ride apart. But the builder of Persepolis was not able to establish a dynasty capable of holding such an empire together for long. In 539 BC Cyrus had taken Babylon; ten years later he died campaigning somewhere near the Oxus river. His grandson Darius I was defeated at Marathon in 490 BC. It was left to his son Xerxes I to defeat the Greeks at Thermopylae, but the Persians were less successful at sea where they lost the battle of Salamis. The Persians never really recovered from this and subsequent defeats at Plataea, Thebes and Mycale, and Xerxes withdrew from military affairs to the softer life of Ecbatana, Persepolis and Susa where he died in the midst of harem intrigues. During the Peloponnesian War the Persians alternated their support between Athens and Sparta, gaining considerably in the process. Finally supporting the Athenians, Artaxerxes was able to dictate the so-called King's Peace of 387 BC. Decline of Persian power in Greece, Anatolia and the eastern Mediterranean then set in and the Empire weakened rapidly. In 331 BC Alexander the Great sacked the

---

The Senate is the upper of two houses which comprise the Iranian Parliament. The building, completed in 1960, was designed by the son of a one-time Prime Minister and shows an interesting merger of an Iranian and European building style

Emamzedah Mir Ahmad, Kashan. It is not only in the larger cities that there are gems of Islamic architecture, but also in the many wayside shrines and religious centres. Similar to that in Kashan is the extremely interesting set of buildings at Bastam, near the city of Shahrud

C

palace and reduced the Empire. It is said that he removed bullion worth more than $200 million.

The culture of the Achaemedians was a mixture of assumed forms—a pattern that can, in itself, be regarded as typical of Persia's development since. The buildings of the Achaemedians were a result of the crafts of many peoples, the languages were as varied as the subject peoples and many individual religions were practised in the country parts. In the cities and amongst the the nobility the teachings of Zoroaster became increasingly popular. Zoroastrianism is all too easily associated with the worship of fire and insufficient attention is normally given to its ethical emphasis on truth and the conflict between God as Ahura Mazda and the lie as personified by Druj. Zoroastrianism was almost certainly practised at Persepolis by Xerxes and even now, 2,500 years later, Zoroastrians number some 40,000 people who are found mainly in and around Yazd.

For almost a century after the destruction of Persepolis, Greece ruled the area now occupied by modern Iran but it was an occupation by a force that assumed more and more of the Persian culture, as marriage and the use of Persian administrators transformed the occupying force. An invasion by Aryan tribes from the north-east in the mid-third century BC brought in the Parthian dynasty and again the invaders became Persianised. For the better part of three centuries the Parthians led the resistance to Roman imperialism in the east. Fighting persisted intermittently throughout the period but the Parthians were never subjected by Rome and the Romans only rarely crossed the Euphrates.

With the adoption of Christianity as the state religion of Rome in the third century AD, Zoroastrianism had become something of a rallying point for the Persian people and some persecution of Christians had taken place under the Sassanians. Early in the seventh century the Persian armies were again at the very gates of Constantinople, while Damascus was occupied in 613, Jerusalem in 614 and Egypt in 619. Such strenuous military campaigns weakened both the Persian and Byzantine empires. The stage was set for the emergence of the Arabs under the banner of Mohammed.

Mohammed had died in 632 at a time when his followers were still confined to a few of the more powerful tribes of Arabia. Spiritual leadership was then vested in the Caliph and terrible struggles followed during the next few decades as the various factions sought to establish their candidates. Some favoured Ali, the Prophet's cousin and husband of his favourite daughter Fatimah, and believed that the Caliphate should be kept in the Prophet's own family—this sect becoming known as the Shi'i. Others favoured succession passing to the most suitable members of the Prophet's tribe, the Omayyad, who later formed the majority sect of the Sunni's. A third group, the Kharejites, believed that the Caliphate should not be based on a hereditary succession but should be allocated on the basis of piety.

Having established their authority over the Bedouin tribes of Arabia, early Caliphs had then to divert the military enthusiasm of their followers away from plundering other, at least nominally, Islamic tribes. A holy war, or *jehad*, was the obvious outlet. 'In the mind of every Arab from Omar (the 3rd Caliph) down to the lowliest soldier, Allah, Mohammed, war booty, tribute, martyrdom and paradise were all part of the indivisible package.'

It was this fiery sword from the deserts of Arabia that fell on the so recently proud Persian Empire, exhausted by its struggle with Greece and in five short years, starting with the battle of Qadesiyeh in 637 and concluding with Nahavand in 641, reduced it to a dependency of Arabia. Probably the Persians have never come to terms with this national catastrophe. Many times has the country been invaded, and the invaders assimilated into the main stream of Persian life. The assimilation of Islam was slower and less successful than other purely racial assimilations and even then was severely modified. The assassination in 680 of the Caliph Hosayn, an almost direct descendant of the Prophet, by a faction of the Omayyad tribe, assumed the character of a martyrdom and became the rallying point for all those of the Faith who were non-Arabs and lived outside Arabia. Shi'ism from then on became the firmly established form of Islam. But the Persians have not forgotten that it was defeat at the hands of the Arabs that brought Islam to Iran, an association which has not been, it would seem, to the advantage of the Faith.

Shi'ism is a speculative religion with overtones of Zoroastrianism and Christianity. It elevated Ali and the eleven Immans to a position of infallibility, something attributed only to the Koran by the Sunni's. With power of infallibility the Immans were given the authority to interpret the Islamic law from which grew rapidly the political system whereby the Immans and legitimate government became inseparable. Like the Christians, the Shi'is believe in the doctrine of the Return: in their Faith it is the 12th Imman, who disappeared in 878 BC, who will return and unite the whole world under the jurisdiction of Shi'i Islam.

In the century that followed Nahavand in 641 it is doubtful if Islam made much impact on Iran. The Omayyad dynasty in Arabia was expressly Sunni in its philosophy and all non-Arabs were prevented from holding senior posts or even entering Arabia. Islamic society became stratified with slaves at the lowest level and above them the Zemmi (members of the tolerated religions such as Judaism and Christianity and later Zoroastrianism) whilst above these were the Mavali who were the non-Arab Moslems. The largest group of these within the Empire were the Persians, frequently known by the Arab word *ajam*. The highest strata were the Arab born Muslims. Zemmi and Mavali were heavily taxed to pay for the Empire and the Holy Wars. Persians had no real loyalty or affection for a system where they were always inferior.

In 750 the ruling Omayyad dynasty was overthrown with the help of a Persian army led by Abu Moslem, and Damascus was sacked. The Abbasid dynasty was established and a greater emphasis was subsequently placed on the beliefs of Islam and a lesser importance attributed to its Arabian origins. Its presence became more obvious to the ordinary Persians who, over the following years, rose in one religious rising after another. Power shifted from one principality to another; boundaries were drawn and redrawn; Saffarids, Samanids and Buyids were followed by the Ghaznavid and Saljug dynasties. If these centuries saw great political upheaval it was also the era of the Iranian Renaissance with men like Razi, Avicenna—Bou Ali of more popular name, whose works on medicine were still read in seventeenth-century Europe—Rudaki, Biruni, Onsori, Farrokhi and, most renowned of all, Ferdowsi whose most famous work was the *Shahnameh*—the *Book of Kings*. Persia demonstrated what other countries have since experienced, that civil strife is a fertile ground for art and culture. Ferdowsi wrote of his own book, 'Much agony did I suffer in these 30 years, but I resurrected Ajam (Iran) with my Persian'.

Of the many small and independent principalities perhaps it was that of Hasan Sabbah (1090–1124) that has most caught the imagination. 'The Old Man of the Mountains' as he was known, ruled from his castle of Alamut in the Elburz Mountains. Here he encouraged the smoking of hashish amongst his followers who subsequently were sent out on numerous murder assignments striking, we are told, fear and terror into all his opponents and extending his power from the Elburz to the Mediterranean. 'He brought a new idea into the political scene of his day', Freya Stark says, 'and treated murder as the suffragette the hunger strike, turning it into an avowed political weapon.' Assassin, a variant on hashish, entered the vocabulary of Europe.

The early thirteenth century marked the beginning of a new era. For centuries Iran and Arabia had been intertwined but the historic connection with central Asia had been moribund. This was dramatically changed in the years after 1220 when Genghiz Khan and his Mongol hordes broke loose from the steppelands of Asia wreaking havoc across vast areas. By 1227, Bokhara, Merv, Nishapur and most of the cities of western Persia had been sacked and some utterly destroyed. Islam and the Persian culture survived 'by the seductive influence which it inevitably had upon the later generations of Mongol rulers'.

The Ilkhans were themselves converted to Islam but encouraged trade and commerce with Christian Europe welcoming the traveller Marco Polo in 1271 and John de Monte Corvino who established a Church in China before 1300. Within a century the central control of the Ilkhans had disappeared and again numerous provincial kingdoms were established to last but a short time before the second Mongol invasion, that of Tamerlane between 1380 and 1393. Savage and barbarous deeds were soon replaced by a policy of restoration of the arts, medicine and learning by Tamerlane's son, Shahrukh.

In 1490, just after the somewhat precarious establishment of the Tudor dynasty in England, a remarkable youth of thirteen, Esma'il, became the leader of the Turkoman Safavi tribe. By the age of twenty-eight, after fifteen years of almost continuous warfare, he was master of all Iran, from the borders of Syria to the Oxus river and from the Caucasian mountains to the Persian Gulf. Esma'il loathed the Sunni's and gave his people the option of conversion to Shi'i, or death. Conversion was rapid, we are told, and almost universal. Cruel and intolerant as this was it united Iran at a crucial time and enabled a united front to be formed against the expanding Ottoman empire. Although he was defeated by Sultan Selim I at Chaldiran in 1514, Esma'il prevented the Turks from annexing Iran to the rule of Constantinople and, despite the nearly 300 years of war that followed, the two empires were never united.

The most famous of the Safavids was Shah Abbas who became Shah in 1587. This was a most propitious time: the Ottoman threat had diminished, the eastern boundary was secure and the demand for silks and spices in Europe led to a great increase in trade with the Orient. Shah Abbas moved his capital from Qazvin to Isfahan and created a city whose wealth and beauty became the stuff of fables. He imported craftsmen from as far as Italy and China; he allowed full religious toleration and encouraged a sizeable settlement of Christian Armenians, traders and craftsmen in Jolfa, a suburb of Isfahan. He invited Pope Clement VIII to send a Christian mission to the city and in 1603 a group of Augustinians arrived to be followed by Carmelites in 1607. He welcomed, with due formality, ambassadors from both east and west. Diplomatic links were established with Queen Elizabeth in England. Legal and administrative reforms were achieved. The country grew rich on trade. History records Shah Abbas as 'bright witted, martial, mercurial, strong, healthy, sagacious in business . . .' In addition, he kept a harem of several hundred women and 'more than 200 boys'. He had succeeded as shah on account of his brother's murder and himself ordered the execution of his three sons lest they should attempt to overthrow him. He kept, it was said, his 500 official executioners 'busy'.

'When Shah Abbas the Great ceased to breathe, Persia ceased to prosper,' wrote Chardin a century later and just prior to the Afghan invasion. An exaggeration no doubt but the succeeding Safavids were a poor stock and the country presented little opposition to the Afghans who won a resounding victory outside Isfahan in 1722. Iran seemed an easy prey for Afghan, Russian and Ottoman territorial aggression and would have been so had not Nader Qoli, from the Afshar tribe, rallied the people and led successful campaigns against the aggressors. Nader became shah in 1736. In the next eleven years he engaged in several more military campaigns—he captured Kabul, Peshawar and Lahore in 1738 and sacked Delhi a year later. He returned with many treasures, including the diamond studded Peacock Throne (now on display in Tehran) and that 'biggest-diamond-of-them-all' the Koh-i-Nor (now part of the British Crown Jewels). A free-thinker himself, he aimed at religious toleration, ordered that the Bible and the Koran be translated into Persian and put forward plans to unite Shia with Sunni. If he had had the time, he is reported as having said, he would have devised a new religion! He shifted his capital to Mashad so that Khorasan should be the centre of his expanded empire, but his true capital, a contemporary remarked, was 'the seat of a saddle and the back of a horse'. His reforms met stiff opposition, he became cruel and suspicious, and murdered his son and was himself assassinated in 1747.

From the sixteenth century onwards Iranian history shows

the growing interest and involvement of European trading and later, imperialistic interests. The Portuguese established trading bases at Hormuz, Muscat and Bahrein in 1514 while the British gained trading rights from Shah Abbas. In 1561 a British representative of the Muscovy Company had reached Qazvin by way of the Caspian Sea. The Dutch East India Company gained additional trading rights to the English from Shah Abbas and it was not until the reign of Nader Shah that the English began to show a clear economic supremacy. To reinforce this the English sent a warship, HMS *Seahorse*, the first ever to sail up the Gulf in 1775; on board was a young midshipman, one Horatio Nelson. The British used Bushehr as their base and the East India Company as their trading agent. In 1783 the Persians lost control of Bahrein.

In 1798 Napoleon occupied Egypt and Syria and began to plan a campaign which would culminate in the conquest of India. Persia was to be conquered first. The threat was never great but it was sufficiently serious to encourage a far greater interest in Persia by Britain, who feared for her Indian Empire, and by Russia, who wanted a 'warm water' port on the southern seas.

An attempt by Persia to recover Georgia was unsuccessful and led to the humiliating treaty of Gulistan in 1813. A further conflict led to still more loss of territory and the treaty of Turkomanci in 1828 and a punitive war indemnity payable to the Russians of £3 million. Persia then turned her attention eastward to the lost territory of Herat and Sistan and in this she was encouraged by the Russians. Britain responded vigorously to what would have been an extension of Russian power on the borders of her Indian empire. Eventually, Persia was forced to admit the existence of an independent—if British puppet—state of Afghanistan established by the Treaty of Paris in 1857. In Sistan a British boundary commission defined a new boundary in 1872 (revised by the McMahon Commission in 1905). The Persians were unlucky, too, in their attempts to reclaim lost territory in Turkestan north of Kopet Dagh and, by the turn of the century, the boundary was established along the lower

Atrek river. Bokhara, Merv and the rich agricultural steppe-lands, went to Russia.

In 1821–3 a war with Turkey had led to minor territorial gains within the Kurdish areas but, despite boundary commissions which inevitably contained British and Russian officials in 1843 and 1874, no clearer boundary than a zone of between 20 and 40 miles (32–64km) stretching from Mt Ararat to the Gulf, could be defined. A further commission in 1914—Anglo-Russian inevitably—led to the contentious issue of the Shat al Arab, not finally resolved until 1975.

British interest in the Gulf during the nineteenth century was dominated by the needs of its Indian Empire. Projected railways linking Europe by means of Persia to India lost the sense of urgency after the opening of Suez in 1875 but the Gulf as an alternative, and shorter, land and water route to India was a well guarded reserve. The British conscience was also involved in anti-slave trade measures by which Belouchis were taken from the Makran to Oman, as well as measures against piracy and gun-running. 'Various political agreements, which did not concern Persia, were made with the Arab states', states the British Admiralty Handbook of 1945. If they did not concern Persia then, they certainly have done since, as the negotiations leading to the formation of the Union of Arab Emirates and the final departure of the British Navy in 1971 showed. Russian interest in persuading Persia to provide her with port facilities on the Gulf forced Britain in 1895 to state that she would resist the attempts of any nation to establish itself on the Gulf and, four years later, the Viceroy of India with an escort of four cruisers paid a state visit to demonstrate '. . . the first duty of Great Britain, the pax Britannica, that now reigns the South Seas in consequence of her temperate control . . .'.

If Britain and Russia had circumscribed Persia's borders during the nineteenth century her internal affairs were no less directed by them. The Indo-European Telegraph Company crossed Persia with its lines in 1870, giving not only communication between London and Delhi but between Persian city and city; political and economic isolation were progressively broken

down by the ease of communications. The British-naturalised
Baron, Julien de Reuter, gained a concession in 1872 for a
monopoly on all railways, road building schemes, irrigation
works, mines, telegraphs, factories and customs duties for
seventy years. The British and Russian governments indulged
in a rare piece of co-operation and forced the Shah to revoke
the concession fearing that de Reuter had gained what would
otherwise have been theirs to take. The Russians established the
only permanent military unit in the country—the Persian
Cossack Brigade—and staffed it entirely with Russian officers.
To balance the Great Powers Britain was granted the Karum
River concession. In 1889 de Reuter was granted a smaller
concession than that for which he had originally aimed, the
establishment of the Imperial Bank of Persia with the power
to print its own money. In 1901 W. K. D'Arcy, an Englishman,
was granted a sixty-year concession for the exploitation of oil
resources. Foreign governments forced what were known as
'capitulations' for their nationals, whereby the Persian government was unable to try them for crimes committed within the
country—a reflection, no doubt, of what the world saw as the
state of Persian justice. Perhaps the most iniquitous scheme
was the Tobacco Regie of 1890 whereby a British company, in
exchange for an annual payment of £15,000 to the Shah, was to
have total control over the production, preparation and sale of
Persian tobacco. The British shareholders were told to expect
profits of half a million pounds a year. Indignation and a well
co-ordinated boycott of tobacco throughout Iran forced the
Shah to revoke this concession as well, but not before the
company had extracted compensation of £500,000.

Nasr-ed-Din had become Shah in 1848 and so had presided
over these great indignities to his country. A fascinating account
of Persia, and of the Shah in particular, is given by Lord
Curzon who, as *The Times* correspondent, wrote *Persia and the
Persian Question* in 1892—the same man in fact who, as Viceroy
of India, visited the Gulf some twelve years later with four
cruisers. Curzon speaks of the Shah as 'the best existing speci-
men of a moderate despot; for within the limits indicated he is

practically irresponsible and omnipotent. He has absolute command over the life and property of every one of his subjects. . . . The sovereign is the sole executive . . . no civil tribunals are in existence to check or modify his prerogative.' His Court was somewhat dowdy and poor in comparison with his illustrious predecessors' but it was still essentially oriental. His harem was thought to number no more than sixty but, with pensions of between £200 and £2,000 a year each, it must have represented at least a financial encumbrance. He had, however, no more than forty children—a moderate man indeed in comparison with his great-grandfather, Fath Ali Shah, to whom 5,000 living descendants were attributed at his death. Shah Nasr-ed-Din was fond of cats: a special carriage was built for one, a pension of £400 a year granted to another whilst another, having fallen asleep on the coat tails of a courtier, the Shah insisted that the coat tails be cut off rather than the cat be disturbed. The Shah was also partial to practical jokes: a collapsible india-rubber boat was presented to him by an English officer and he ordered a dozen of his ADCs and chamberlains to row out in this on a pond in the royal garden, the Shah having first secretly removed the valve. The spectacle of these richly dressed grandees floundering in the water is said to have given the Shah 'intense amusement'.

Shah Nasr-ed-Din was assassinated in 1896 but his successor was no less incompetent. Mozaffar al-Din was amiable, ineffective and sufficiently sickly to persuade his ministers that he would have to travel to Europe to be cured. The country was penniless and a loan of £3·4 million was raised from the Russians—a figure equivalent to twice the national income. A second European tour necessitated a further loan of £1 million granted, again by Russians, in return for a concession on all the roads in north Persia. Later the British made a loan of £300,000 at 5 per cent per annum, on the security of the Caspian fisheries for twenty years.

The Persian people could take no more. The Persian paper, *Qanum*, published in London in the 1890s said:

the control of State affairs is in the hands of ignorant and base born men . . . . the rights of the State are bartered to please legation drago-mans . . . Our army is the laughing stock of the world . . . our priests and learned clergy crave the justice of the infidels . . . our princes deserve the pity of beggars . . . our towns are each a metro-polis of dirt . . . our roads are worse than the tracks of animals. . . .

In December 1905 a group of merchants, in desperation following yet a further increase in the taxation on sugar to meet the royal debts, closed the bazaar—by Persian standards an event of great magnitude. The Shah had the merchants flogged, the demonstrations grew larger; the Shah partially relented, and then went back on his word. In July 1906 all the clergy withdrew from Tehran and took *baast* (sanctuary) in Qum and some twelve thousand Tehrani businessmen and other leaders of the community took *baast* in the grounds of the British Legation, certainly it would seem, with the support of the British. The Shah, finding that the British were supporting the demonstration, agreed to grant a Constitution and authorised the formation of a National Assembly, or *Majlis*. Rejoicings were short-lived. Within six months the Shah died and his son, Mohammed Ali, well known as a puppet of the Russians, suc-ceeded to the throne. The Russian Tsar's own experience of a constitution had led him to dissolve the *Duma* as soon as it had been elected; this is just what the new Shah tried to do. He appointed an arch reactionary as prime minister who was assas-sinated shortly afterwards by a terrorist with mixed anti-monarchist and constitutionalist sympathies. Tehran was thrown into confusion. The confusion was compounded by the discovery of a secret Anglo-Russian convention which sought to define the Great Powers' spheres of interest in Iran; dismay quickly gave way to disgust that the British who, in the previous year, had supported the Constitution, could behave in such a cynical fashion.

The Shah ordered the Cossack Brigade to bombard the *Majlis*. Risings occurred in Tabriz and Rasht. Armed Bakhtiaris marched on Tehran. Civil war raged throughout 1909.

Eventually the Shah took *baast* in the Russian Legation and abdicated in favour of the young Sultan Ahmad. The war ended and a new *Majlis* was convened. Two parties emerged: the Social Democrats, who were revolutionary and inspired by European idealism, and the Social Moderates, whose concern was to remove the abuses of the existing system. Both parties were unanimous in pressing for a solution to the immediate financial and legal problems. America was asked to provide financial advice and Morgan Shuster of the US Treasury began work in May 1911. Adolphe Perni, a French lawyer, was commissioned to produce a new penal code. Shuster worked fast. He reorganised the tax system, challenged the right of Iranians to take *baast* in foreign legations and so avoid tax, and generally inspired a new sense of confidence amongst the deputies. This displeased the Russians, who demanded his removal. Two more ultimatums were sent, now supported by the British, and eventually Shuster was dismissed. Faith in Britain fell to a new low.

Persia declared herself neutral when World War I was declared but, inevitably, this was not respected. Prior to the Russian Revolution the Tzarist armies were occupied in campaigns against the Turks which involved action on Persian territory around Lake Urmia. British troops occupied parts of Khuzistan to protect the oil wells and other installations against tribal attacks fermented by Turkish and German agents. With the withdrawal of Russian troops after the October Revolution British troops had moved into north-west Persia to prevent a possible Turko-German invasion as a spearhead for a drive on India.

Fearing the imperial interests of both Russia and Great Britain, Persian sympathies were, initially, with the Axis powers. A number of extreme nationalists set up revolutionary governments in Azerbaijan, Gilan and Khorasan. Chief amongst their leaders was Kuchek Khan, and his troops, the Jangali. In the Russian Revolution they saw the possible end of Russian imperialism and made common cause with the Bolsheviks. A Russian Autonomous Soviet Republic was established for a few short months in Gilan in 1920.

The majority of the Persian moderates, however, feared the effects of the Revolution and the growth of Communism. Great Britain exploited this situation and began subsidising the Persian Government with a quarter of a million pounds a month and plans were formulated—by Lord Curzon, now Foreign Secretary—for a new Anglo-Persian treaty that would have placed Persia firmly within the orbit of British tutelage. Opposition from America and from the constitutionalists led to the rejection of this treaty at the last moment. Prime Minister Vosug fell and was replaced by Mushir al-Doleh, who looked not to Britain but to the Bolsheviks for support and signed the Iran-Soviet treaty of 1921. Having received this rebuff, the British interest in Persia took another form and evidence suggests some British complicity in the moves which led to the coup d'état of 1921. Certainly, strong government was preferable, in British eyes, to a weak Russian-dominated regime. Seyyed Ziya who, with Reza Khan, led the coup is thought to have had close dealings with the British Legation staff. Very much a theorist and not possessing sufficient personal qualities for leadership, he resigned as prime minister after only three months and then fled the country. Reza Khan became Prime Minister two years later, having served his apprenticeship as Minister of War and having gained the allegiance of the majority of Persians for his firm and capable handling of domestic problems. There was talk of a Republic as Ahmad Shah became more unpopular. Reza Khan played his cards well. He sided with the chief clergy in Qum (a rare event indeed!) against such an idea and, when the *Majlis* deposed the *Qajar* dynasty on 31 October 1925, it was only days before the Constitution was amended and Reza Khan declared Reza Shah Pahlavi on 12 December 1925. Only four deputies had the courage to oppose this move. One was Dr Mossadegh who said that it was a shame to promote an active prime minister to the inactive position of shah . . .!

4

How the Country is Run

THE Shah runs Iran. He is Shah in as complete and as absolute a fashion as any one of his ancestors. Some of his people adulate him, some fear, some loathe, but most are glad that he is there and are prepared to enjoy the fruits of what he has created without thinking too much about the base on which it is all built, or what the future may bring. Personally, his career is one of rags to riches, but he has identified himself and his career so closely with that of the country that this, too, is the story of Iran. At the age of fifty-eight his thoughts are, inevitably, turning to retirement and old age. Simplistically, he sees before him a new, revitalised Iran; an Iran that he has rescued from oblivion and returned to the traditions of Darius.

Mohammed Reza Pahlavi has been Shah for a long time; longer than any other monarch alive today and far, far longer than any president or prime minister. His survival has at no time been guaranteed. The throne which he ascended in 1941 could have been overthrown on many occasions. The assassin's bullet has come precious near to killing him. The mob from the bazaar could have deposed him. Communism could have progressively swamped the country. The West could have milked the oil industry dry. His survival depends increasingly on his political and ecnomic acumen as well as on a secret police, the *savak*, reputedly among the most effective in the world.

Historians may well see distinct chapters in the Shah's life, as psychologists may detect reactions, complexes and over reactions in the way in which he, and the country, have changed.

As a boy he was very much under the influence of a stern, some say ogrelike, father and lived an austere life in a country that seemed to have no future alongside the wealthy giants of the West. The West he began to appreciate when sent to school in Switzerland. For long years after his accession Iran was still a land of immensely wealthy aristocrats to whom the Pahlavi's were upstarts, chancers and dangerous revolutionaries. His country was almost unknown. 'Where do you come from?' asked the milkman at his Swiss school.

'Persia', the young crown prince replied.

'Oh yes, I have heard of Persia', the reply came, 'that's in America!'

The sense of destiny was felt when still young but he knew that the path ahead would be lonely. It has been. The Shah allows himself but few close friends. His destiny, as he sees it, is to put the name and reality of Iran amongst the nations of the world and the name and reality of the Shah on the lips of all Iranians. No milkman now would place Persia in America, no Iranian is unaware of the Shah, but neither is necessarily grateful for the change.

The opening years of the Shah's reign were not auspicious. His country was occupied by the two powers who, for a century

---

Mohammed Reza Shah Pahlavi dam. Completed in 1962, this dam on the Dez river has the largest capacity of any of the Iranian storage schemes. Many other dams are in the course of construction. 4m hectares of land are now being irrigated, but currently plans are being made to increase this to 18m hectares. The production of HEP is being expanded rapidly

A school laboratory. The expansion of education has been a major priority during recent years. The number of pupils has increased from 2·1 million in 1963 to 7·7 million in 1976. The provision of new buildings and equipment has been difficult, but a greater difficulty has been the training of efficient teachers to meet this new demand

and a half, had been meddling in Iranian affairs and with whom, years later, he was to do serious business. It was touch and go in the late 1940s as to whether the Autonomous Socialist Republic of Azerbaijan could be put down, while in the 1953 riots he had to flee the country. The lesson learnt then was a hard one and one which many have had cause to rue since. Darius had established an elaborate spy network—'The King has many ears, and many eyes', says an ancient Persian proverb —and when the Shah returned following Mossadegh's over-throw, the advice of the CIA and the Mossad was taken in forming *savak*—*Sazemane Attalat Va Amniyate Keshvar* (National Organisation for Information and Security). The Shah was then thirty-three years old. The Americans became more willing to offer him support; so too were other countries. He used this support, but continued to go his own way. Greater maturity bred greater confidence. Land reform was essential if Iran was to throw off the bondage of feudalism and essential, too, if the Shah was to be really ruler of his own country.

The majority of the land of Iran was in the hands of some 1,000 families, by far and away the largest holdings being those of the Crown and the Islamic Church. A number of measures were promulgated in 1961 and 1962 but the *Majlis*, dominated

———

The smoking of the hooka is still widespread amongst country people

Tea remains the universal drink. It is offered at all times of the day and is a sign of acceptance for a stranger. The tea is bitter, taken without milk, while sugar lumps are placed, not in the tea glass, but directly in the mouth and the tea sucked over them

D

by the land owning class, refused to make this law. Eventually, the Shah dissolved the *Majlis* and ruled by decree, choosing as his Prime Minister Assadollah Alam, an aristocrat from Khorasan and one-time Governor of Baluchestan. 600 decrees were promulgated before the *Majlis* was reconvened. In January 1963 a congress of farmers was summoned in Tehran. At this the Shah, before an audience of 5,000 farmers ('you represent 75 per cent of the population', the Shah told them), the Diplomatic Corps, together with all the governors who had been especially summoned to Tehran, announced that he would hold a national referendum at the end of the month on the land reform bill and five other reform bills. These were the nationalisation of forests, the sale of Government factories to finance land reform, the factory workers' profit-sharing plan, the Literacy Corps and a revised electoral law which allocated greater powers to the farmers. Just before the referendum it was announced that women could vote. The official voting figures showed nearly 6 million in favour and a mere 4,000 against but nevertheless these measures were not readily accepted. Opposition came from the clergy, the left wing and the land owning and business classes. June 1963 saw street risings in Tehran and other cities, with martial law being introduced. Opposition from tribal chiefs was particularly strong. The Shah had been on the throne for twenty-two years when these measures were introduced. To the original package six other reforms were added: the Health Corps, the Extension and Development Corps, Houses of Justice, Nationalisation of Water, Urban and Rural Reconstruction and Education and Administrative Reforms. These became the 'Twelve points of the White Revolution' or, as it is now known, the Shah-People Revolution.

The break with the old *Majlis* had been essential if the Shah was to triumph over the feudal elements which had previously dominated the Government. The elections which were held in June 1963 and those held subsequently, at least up to 1975, were in no real sense 'free' and the *Majlis* has not emerged as the powerful democratic instrument of government that the

Constitution would suggest that it should. The Shah has expressed many times in recent years his disillusionment with democratic processes, at least in as far as they are practised in the West.

The choice of Persepolis for the 2,500th Celebrations was surely, as has been suggested before, symbolic? Increasingly, the Shah has been thinking in terms of the greatness of his country, measured in terms that are pre-Islamic, grandiose and expansionist. Asked by a BBC correspondent what he most admired of Old Persia, the Shah replied 'The humanitarisation of the Persian spirit. We have always treated the people of different creeds and religions in a very equal way; this country has always been a haven for all those people . . . so that I would like to see this continued and the philosophy of our forefathers which has been expressed so beautifully in the books, in the poems, in the poetry, because by modernising they still will hold the spiritual aspect of the human being and value it as much as they should, and that is to mix spirit with naturalistic things.' The Shah's experience of the *mullahs* (priests) has not been fortunate, though he claims not to dislike them as much as his father did. In his own way the Shah is religious: at an early age he saw visions—dreams and aspirations is how he now describes them. 'I believe that I am protected; this is the reason why I am still here. I have got to accomplish a job and I am helped in my job by these supernatural powers—that I believe . . . I am mystical.' Is it to an earlier understanding of God, than that revealed by Mohammed, that the Shah turns? When he renamed the Mohammedan year 1355 2535 (March 1976) Premier Hoveyda was quick to explain to the *Majlis* that this would not abolish the existing religious calendar but that '. . . your decision today is indeed a reflection of the historic fact that during this long period there has been only one Iran, and one monarchical system . . . (which) provide a sense of what Iran will achieve in the future on the road towards the Great Civilisation.'

If the Shah is 'mystical', he is also puritancial. He has been, and is, a prodigiously hard worker. He reads the world's leading daily newspapers, studies reports—'After thirty-five years' experience . . . I don't need to read ten pages before I know what it's all about'—and works a fourteen-hour day. He eats but little (no caviar) and drinks in moderation. 'If each person asks himself when he rises from sleep in the morning, or before going to bed at night "Have I performed the task that had to be done, and paid back the debt owed to my country?" I do not think there is anything else that I should say (to my people).' His Queen is his third wife—but only because of the need for a male successor. He takes great delight, as do all Iranians, in his family. He takes family holidays at Ramsar on the Caspian, where he has a palace, or at St Moritz, where he has a villa.

The Shah-People Revolution gave the Shah and Iran much on which to build but, as the years have passed, the Shah has felt the need to project forward rather than to look back. 'The Great Civilisation' is now a matter of daily concern and discussion. The vast wealth that accrued to Iran following the increased price of oil in 1973 made more possible the plans and aspirations of the Shah to put Iran on a par with Europe, within what he expects to be his own lifetime. 'If things progress the way they do now, in twelve years we might catch up on what Europe is today. And in one generation, say twenty-five years' time, we'll be among the advanced countries of the world' (1976).

The increase in wealth has been prodigious. The annual budget, presented in December 1973 but drawn up before the oil price rise, was for $10·1 billion, a rise of 32 per cent over that for the previous year, but later revised to $16·1 billion. In December 1974 Premier Hoveyda presented a budget for $30·1 billion and promised a budget of $36·2 billion for the year 1975–6. With increased wealth forward planning has become the more essential. The first plan, for seven years, was produced by Premier Razmara in 1950, but proved to be a disaster. The present five-year plan, the fifth, started on 21 March 1973. It was originally scheduled to have a total investment of $32 billion, a rise in per capita income from $513 to $907 and a growth rate of 11·4 per cent. Six months later the economists, having redone their calculations in the light of higher oil revenues, Plan and Budget Organisation (PBO) laid a revised plan before the Shah for a total investment of $68·6 billion, a rise in per capita income to $1,600 and a growth rate of 26 per cent. '. . . this Plan will prove to be the spearhead of one of the country's most brilliant and successful transformations . . . and guide Iran more rapidly to the period of the Great Civilisation', said Majidi, Head of PBO.

The early euphoria which this bred was somewhat dulled by the reduced demand for oil and the consequent fall in revenues, as well as what the Shah bitterly calls 'imported inflation'. Stressing that the increase in the price of oil accounted for no more than inflation of 2 per cent, the Shah threatened an increase of 30 per cent in oil prices to compensate for the increased cost of the manufactured goods which he was buying. Market forces worked against this and September 1975 saw a more moderate increase of 10 per cent. By 1976 it was becoming obvious that Iran would have to finance its long term projects with some international loans. Will the Western world have sufficient confidence 'in the continuing stability of Iran to provide long term loans at reasonable rates?', wrote Lord Chalfont in *The Times*. 'The Shah's autocratic grip on his country's political and economic life carries its own built-in weakness . . . in spite of the draconian efficiency of the Iranian security services, the life of any national leader is at the mercy of a really determined assassin.'

As years have passed the Shah has come to expect less and less limitation on his actions. An expanding financial base, a more secure social and economic structure to society, greater experience of the international scene—all of these it would seem have tempted the Shah to assert a position that many find objectionable. The Shah is frustrated from both within and without. Not all Iranians share the same goals, nor do they have the same idealistic approach to their country's destiny. The breakneck speed with which economic growth has been achieved has left the political growth of the country far behind.

The moral leadership of the *mullahs* was further undermined by the events of 1963 and Islamic Iran seems lost in the spiritual and philosophical turmoil that now places Iran somewhere between East and West. A sense of destiny guides the Shah, a puritanical background colours some of his actions, but the ordinary Iranian is either hell bent on absorbing as much of the material wealth of his country as he can, or is critical of a political system which he does not accept.

Between 1958 and 1960 the Shah wrote a history-cum-autobiography: *Mission for my Country*. It was written while the White Revolution was only an unstructured dream and before the riches of Croesus projected Iran into a nightmare of activity. *Savak* was almost unknown. One of the chapters is entitled 'Democracy as I see it'; it now makes fascinating reading. 'Through much painful experience men have found that genuine individual freedom can be obtained only through the democratic system, which allows ordinary people actually to control the society in which they live,' the Shah wrote. Experience showed, the Shah noted, that political stability does not necessarily follow economic growth and that planned economic and political evolution must go 'hand in hand'. When this was written the Shah could not have foreseen what problems would follow with the economic growth rate of his own country a generation later.

Party politics is something new to Iran. In its simplest terms the Shah would like the people to be politically involved, but only if their views conform with his overall strategy. True democracy only comes, as he has frequently said, with a politically educated populace and a pre-requisite of this is, presumably, a literate population. In late 1976 62 per cent of Iranians were still illiterate. The Shah has instructed his politicians to develop a 'national debate' to involve all the people in planning for the future. The Shah is suspicious, and rightly so, of outside interference in his country's affairs and is extremely sceptical of the so-called 'democratic face' that such external powers try to develop. The UK and USSR both dictated to his Parliament during the war years while the Tudeh (Communist) party received full backing from the USSR, both in the setting up of the Azerbaijan Republic and during subsequent years. At present, relations with the Soviet Union are cordial, as are those with the West. But what started off as a fear of communism has now spread to any form of criticism and alternatives, be they of the left or of the right. The Shah has established a state where he is supreme ruler and where he is fed with ideas and schemes from his own PBO, the criticism of which is seen as being tantamount to criticism of himself.

Until 1975 the majority party was Iran Novin, led by Premier Hoveyda. It had held power since the *Majlis* was reconvened in 1963. The Mardon Party, with 37 of the 268 seats in the *Majlis* was condemned to a minority role. Suspicion was cast on the way in which the candidates were nominated and later elected. The Shah had charged the Mardon Party with the role of 'active criticism', but closely associated himself with Iran Novin. It was a brave, and not particularly wise man, therefore, that associated himself with Mardon. In November 1974 the Mardon Secretary-General Nasser Ameri was severely critical of a number of aspects of the present Government. 'The ruling Iran Novin party saw administrative reform as a threat to its own interests', he said, and called for a campaign against corruption. He stated that the next election must be conducted entirely impartially, that Government officials should not interfere and that they should not use public funds to win votes. Despite an assurance given in June 1973 'that Iran will not be administered on the basis of the single party system, which usually leads to dictatorship', just such a move was made in March 1975. A new party, Rastakhiz, or Resurgence, was formed and all active, recognised parties were invited to join. *The Times* had commented on the previous election when Mardon had gained 10·7 per cent of the votes, that this constituted 'the collapse of the Shah's efforts to create a two-party system in Iran'. The newspaper reminded its readers of the Shah's comments, reported in *The New Republic* in December 1973. When asked what he thought of 'a regime that allows everyone to think as they wish and is based on a Parliament where even minorities are represented', the Shah had replied, 'But I don't want that kind of democracy! Haven't you understood that? I don't know what to do with that kind of democracy! I don't want any part of it . . .'.

Despite official reports of 'enthusiasm' the new party does not appear to have stirred popular imagination. In an interview with Danish Television in June 1976 the Shah was questioned about why, having given a commitment to a two-party system, he had in fact reversed his position. He replied

> *. . . Because in a country developing like our own country, and while fulfilling the wishes of the people . . . the party in power would always win at the polls . . . it was becoming most pathetic to see very nice, very brilliant people in the opposition losing just because they belonged to the opposition party. By creating this party, in fact, we have permitted within this party any number of ideas, opinions, proposals to be expressed. So within this party we have more than a two-party system, . . . we have maybe 10, 15, 20 different shades of ideas and opinions. So it's just a question of façade, but the reality is that we have much more possibility of expression now than when we had the two-party system.*

Mr Hoveyda was appointed Secretary General of the new party. Two senior members of Government, Jamshid Amuzgar the Minister of the Interior, and Hushang Ansari the Minister of Finance, were appointed to form the two 'wings' in the party—Amuzgar, the Progressive Liberals and Ansari, the Constructive Liberals. The elections for the twenty-fourth session of the *Majlis* were held only six months after the party reorganisation. Some 900 candidates were selected from 7,000 interested persons to compete for 268 seats. Official figures show that 6·8 million people voted. The experience of this election has prompted demands for widespread reform, not least the need to break up Tehran into constituencies instead of expecting each voter to choose twenty-seven names from a long list of candidates which is the practice at present.

Increasingly, the activities of *Savak* are being brought to the world's attention. Statistics about the organisation are, not surprisingly, hard to discover and those which are available are hard to evaluate. *Kayhan* took the unusual step of republishing, in October 1974 the full text of an article that had appeared a few days earlier in *Newsweek* concerning the activities of *Savak*. This article suggested that the number of full-time agents is between 30,000 and 60,000, 'but they are only the skeleton of a much larger centre. According to some diplomats in Iran, no fewer than three million Iranians are occasional *Savak* informers'. *Savak* is everywhere: 'hotels, taxis, schools, foreign embassies and companies, factories, doctors' offices,' and amongst Iranian students at home and abroad. The number of political prisoners is undoubtedly immense; estimates vary, with the Shah saying that there are fewer than 3,000 in prison for 'terrorist' actions, and exiled opposition groups giving figures ranging from 25,000 to 100,000. Torture is undoubtedly used and execution is not uncommon. The intention is to gain recantations and public declarations of future loyalty to the Shah. The Shah will only admit to certain aspects of this '. . . because the new modern system of questioning people is in itself a kind of torture but it is very refined and a pyschological way of torturing people with your subtle questions'. Amnesty International estimated that there have been 300 executions since 1972; the Iranians said, in July 1974, that the figure was 239, mainly 'drug-pushers, police killers and bank robbers'. Hardly a week passes but the Iranian press announces shoot-outs in Tehran and elsewhere of 'terrorists'.

Opposition to the Shah comes from many areas: religious venom certainly inspires considerable opposition amongst the Shi'a traditionalists while Islamic-Marxists, Marxists, Maoists and ultra-conservative groups are all involved. The most vocal groups are obviously those outside Iran and demonstrations by Iranian students against the regime in their home countries take place with some degree of regularity in Western capitals. Irrefutable evidence, however, exists of *Savak* activities outside Iran where close surveillance is kept on all dissident voices. In September 1976 the Swiss Government requested the removal of an Iranian diplomat whose work involved 'security functions'.

The Shah does not just rely on *Savak*. He must be constantly haunted by the memory of General Bakhtiar, his first head of *Savak*, who was sacked and exiled in 1962 and mysteriously shot five years later when 'a massive plot' against the Shah was unearthed. General Nassiri is currently in charge, having taken over from General Pakravan, who was pensioned off as Ambassador to Afghanistan. Also advising the Shah on security matters is the Special Intelligence Bureau, which is separate from *Savak* and reports direct to him and, also reporting personally is the Army's crack intelligence corps. The shadows of Evin prison stretch across the country and well outside its borders. As the *Newsweek* article concluded: 'Ultimately, however, it is *Savak*'s domestic operations that stir the strongest emotions. But, because of *Savak*'s mercilessness, those emotions are seldom publicly voiced in Iran itself. As one Tehran resident puts it: "In speaking of the Shah, you do not raise your voice. The *Savak* may be listening".'

The Shah finds the West, and the Western press in particular, hard to tolerate. Exercising such wideranging control over his country he finds it hard to understand how Britain, France, Germany, America amongst others do not follow suit and the more rapidly sort out their problems. Increasingly, Iran is indulging in international trade pacts, closely resembling good old-fashioned barter deals. The French have been the quickest to see the advantage of these; the British find them harder to accept. Whatever he may say about worker share ownership, there is no doubt who can, at the touch of a royal signature, direct Iranian industry. But when BP does not take up all its quota option on oil or Chrysler UK is strike-bound and so does not deliver all its spare parts for Peykan cars, it is no use, with respect, for the Shah to blame the Queen or Mr Callaghan. The Shah is quick to tell the West what he thinks. 'Keep your promises, Monarch tells West' was the headline in March 1976 when the Shah found himself in cash flow difficulties over the need to honour a loan agreement that he had made previously with the National Water Council in Britain. Lord Chalfont wrote in *The Times*:

> *If anyone is interested in a little plain speaking about the state of Western civilisation in general and of Britain in particular, I can strongly recommend an evening with the Shah . . . But to be his guest especially if you happen to be British, is a memorable experience, not to say downright salutary if you subscribe to the conventional belief of the island race that to be born British is to have won first prize in the lottery of life . . .*

The headmaster whose patience has nearly been exhausted, some have said, lecturing a lazy but affable and potentially clever pupil, is the Shah's attitude towards many western European states. He told Danish Television reporter Ole Sippel in June 1976:

> *It stems from a lack of discipline. People got tired after World War II. Europe suffered a lot. Then there was that fantastic affluence in the European standard of living, when by exploiting the wealth of the developing countries of the world you people got rich and fat . . . What's wrong with you? Wherever are you to go? Where are you willing to go? Why are you destroying yourselves? For what? With what are you going to replace the old 'white' or Christian civilisation that we know?*

The Shah has not had a good Press in the West recently. From the excesses of *Private Eye* to the secret-police hunts of the Sunday papers, the Shah has appeared in a light which, while the Confederation of Iranian Students might say was still too mild, frequently fails to do justice to what the Shah has achieved or take into account the background against which this has happened. His wilder outbursts are easily derided. *Savak* and a vast military presence are a threat both internally and possibly externally, but the achievements are very real.

THE ROYAL FAMILY

Two women help immensely to humanise the Shah's regime: his twin sister, Princess Ashraf, and his wife, the Empress Farah. Princess Ashraf is one of the very few people that the Shah trusts and that makes her a very powerful figure. She stayed with her brother after her father was deposed. She is as tough and determined as the Shah and she works prodigiously hard. She leads Iran's delegation to the United Nations and presided over the 1975 International Women's Year Conference. She has personally supervised those sections of the 1963 Revolution which deal with literacy, health, population, women and human rights. She is indefatigable in her travels around the country, she exhorts women to still greater efforts, but she is as inflexible as the Shah in her attitude towards terrorists—'It is right to execute them'.

Empress Farah is beautiful, and graceful—and counts for a great deal. Twenty years younger than the Shah, she gave him the heir and the family which two previous wives did not achieve. Like the Princess, she is indefatigable in her travels and in presiding over conferences and 'High Councils'. 'What are your problems?' she says with a disengaging naivety as she meets endless delegations of villagers and women's organisations. She appears with the Shah on most occasions and, as he ages, her help in this respect will be the more important. She seems more aware of the pressures, the aspirations—and the fears—of the ordinary Iranian as, indeed, she is better able to do, having grown up in a traditional Persian home. She takes an especial interest in the role of women and cultural activities. She was educated at the Jeanne d'Arc School in Tehran where she learnt, in the Shah's words, 'added respect for such values as honesty, reliability and punctuality'.

The Crown Prince was born in October 1960. Unlike his father's, his education has been entirely in Iran. There are four children. As with all Iranian children, his early education was entirely within the family. Recently the Shah has been more specific about his own future intentions, talking in terms of handing over office in the late 1980s so that he could be on hand afterwards to give advice if necessary. His son, the Shah has said, must be 'kind in principle; tough against evil things like corruption, enemies of the country . . . understanding towards all, forgiving when it is possible . . . in addition to his being learned, and that he will be very natural and be himself'. There can be few, if any, boys of seventeen who are being so consciously groomed for greatness as is Prince Reza. Fortunately, he is like any healthy boy of his age, interested in hunting, soccer and other non-regal activities. But these are being forced on him at a very early age. He accompanied President Sadaat on the first ship through the reopened Suez Canal in June 1975, he made an official tour of Belgium and the USSR during the summer holidays of 1976, but he 'fully appreciates his position and responsibility as heir to the Peacock Throne, and to one of the key positions in the world . . .', said his parents in May 1976.

DEFENCE

The Shah's spending on defence has reached astronomic proportions. A massive increase in expenditure on arms of 41 per cent in the two years 1975–6 now means that defence accounts for over 28 per cent of the national budget, a figure ($8·18 billion) far higher than the expenditure on all social affairs and four times the size of that spent on agriculture. It is the highest figure in the Middle East and 50 per cent higher than that spent by Israel. It is a higher percentage of the GNP than any Nato or, as far as can be discovered, Warsaw Pact country.

Very little is said, officially, within Iran about the cost of defence. The matter is not debated by the *Majlis*. The presence of the Armed Services, while being kept in moderately low profile, is nevertheless obvious. The Armed Services work in close co-operation with internal security, ex-serving officers, in particular staffing the *Savak* courts.

There are now some quarter of a million men in the ground staff of the Armed Services—a far cry from the 3,000 of the Cossack Brigade at the start of the Pahlavi era. National Service is compulsory for two and a half years, although the edicts of 1963 and subsequent Shah-People Revolution legislation mean that many people move into advisory posts in the literacy, medical and other corps after an initial six months' basic training. Iran now has 2,000 Chieftain tanks (twice as many as Britain herself can afford). In 1975 a multi-million pound contract was signed with Britain for the construction of a new ordnance factory near Isfahan and a $500 million contract was signed with the US Rockwell Foundation for a highly complex computer linked intelligence system that would involve ex-CIA agents, as well as the use of C130 Hercules planes equipped with complex listening devices. It is thought that Iran also has 100 F4 Phantom and 100 F-5A fighter bombers and is taking delivery of a further 70 Phantoms, 140 F-5Es, 80 Grumman F-14s and 300 light attack jets. Iran has the largest fleet of Hovercraft in the world. In addition to the British Chieftain, there are American M-47s and M-60s as well as British Scorpions, which could amount to a total of 5,000 very modern tanks by 1980. Recently 3 submarines and 6 missile destroyers have been added to the Navy. In April 1974 Iran asked Britain to train 145 Iranian naval officers a year at Dartmouth, which has facilities for only 300 in total of whom, in the past, less than eighty have been foreigners.

The West has responded rapidly to the Shah's wish to spend his oil revenues on defence and to link this expenditure with long-term agreements for the supply of oil. If Iran has consciously tried to justify this in terms other than the Shah's anti-Communist stand, it has been a very obvious wish to fill the strategic vacuum left in the Gulf and Indian Ocean area caused by British withdrawal from the Gulf in 1971.

But other questions are now being asked. Has the West allowed itself to become too tied to Iranian arms deals? Could it resist the Shah's demands for more arms without upsetting its own industries? What of the Shah's purchase of 25 per cent of

Krupps and a further interest in the American Grumman Corporation? *Newsweek*, in 1974, reported some Washington observers as being worried by the arms sales. 'The Shah's power is growing. We may be creating a Frankenstein monster. With his egomania and his expansionist vision of revival of ancient Persia's power, the Shah could create a very unstable situation.' (The Shah very naturally did not like this report nor the BBC Television programme that suggested that all this machinery was useless without the western technicians to operate it.) Since then the expenditure on arms has grown at a still greater rate.

The Shah says that his armed forces are necessary to protect his trade routes, particularly the Straits of Hormuz. 'We know very well of the weakness of the United Nations today. A weak country could be subdued, submerged, invaded without the world reacting. This is not going to happen to us.' The Shah and western observers are worried about what would happen to the oil-rich sheikdoms on the Persian Gulf if pan-Arabian radicals took over in order to make political trouble for Israel. There was trouble with Iraq until the cynical Algiers Agreement of March 1975 traded the future of the Kurds for the frontier adjustment on the Shatt al Arab. There is the 1,600km border with the USSR and further land borders with Pakistan and India. No one disputes that the Shah has a national security problem, but but does it really need armed forces as great as those which have now been accumulated? Could not the problem, as many observers suggest, be one of an increasing internal security risk? In the meantime, concern about the size of the military might of Iran increases, America being particularly worried about the scale of the arms shipments thought to amount to 50 per cent of all her overseas sales. The Shah's outbursts seem to have become the more militaristic—'Aggression will be fought to the last man' and 'Monarch outlines total national war strategy'. But against whom?

GOVERNMENT

The Constitution which was granted in 1906 was modelled on those of European democracies but contains special provisions relating to the Islamic religion. It divides government into the three traditional units of executive, legislative and judicial. The Constitution has been amended three times—in 1925, 1949 and 1969. The Shah has the absolute power to appoint or dismiss ministers and to call or dissolve Parliament.

The legislative power is vested in the National Consultative Assembly, known as the *Majlis*, and the Senate. Currently there are 267 members of the *Majlis* and 60 members of Senate, the numbers in the *Majlis* being in the ratio of 1:100,000 of the population, in theory at least, as the present population of 34 million would necessitate a larger body. That there is room for reform of the electoral system has already been noted. According to the Constitution, only the *Majlis* may debate and vote on financial matters. Half the members of the Senate are appointed by the Shah, while half are elected. In April 1974 Jamshid Amouzgar was appointed Minister of the Interior. A man with no previous party political attachment, he was particularly charged by the Shah to prepare for new elections which were to be really free, unbiased and impartially administered. It was well known, both inside and outside Iran, that previous elections had been 'controlled'.

Power, however, lies not with the *Majlis*, but with the executive, in the persons of the Cabinet ministers. The prime minister is, at least technically, chosen by Parliament and then appointed by the Shah. He is answerable to Parliament, who could remove him by a vote of no-confidence. Prior to the appointment of Mr Hoveyda in 1965 there had been thirty-eight prime ministers since the first parliamentary cabinet appointed in 1907 and no fewer than 112 cabinets. Hoveyda's longevity, therefore, is the first matter of consideration and marks the far more stable conditions that have grown up in recent years.

The *Majlis* is a consultative body and it is not necessary for the members of the Cabinet to be drawn from its elected ranks. They rarely are. Hoveyda is not a deputy and never has been. He is both tough and hard and drives others to be the same. As chief minister to the Crown he has always served the Shah well. His father was a diplomat and is remembered by his son as a strict disciplinarian; he died when Hoveyda was ten and with limited finances Hoveyda had to work his way through university. He studied under Spaak in Brussels and when World War II started became an ambulance driver for the Belgian Red Cross. He arrived back in Iran in 1941 and suffered the indignity of having his passport checked on arrival in Ahvaz by a British officer. Various posts in the army and the diplomatic service followed; he gained a PhD while in Paris. When Mansur became Prime Minister in 1964 Hoveyda was offered the job of Finance Minister. 'To be frank I hardly knew what I was expected to do as Finance Minister. I stayed awake every night and read documents and reports studying the job I was to do.' On the assassination of Mansur he became Premier himself. Since then he has seen Iran develop more rapidly than any of his predecessors. He describes himself as 'a man in peace with himself. My blood-pressure is quite normal and I can shut my mind to all pressures at will. I don't believe in fate or things like that.' He finds it difficult to maintain ordinary friendly relations even 'with my old pals'. There could be no room for a colourful, attractive chief deputy to the Shah—and no one would see such a man in Hoveyda, which is probably one of the reasons why he is so good at his job. A position not found in a Western democracy is that of the Minister of Court. The occupant of this post, Assadollah Alam, the Prime Minister in the critical period 1962–3, is an aristocrat and lifelong friend of the Shah. All matters of Court, and much else besides, are dealt with efficiently and graciously by him and on his judgment the Shah is known to act.

The ministers in the Cabinet—there are twenty-five of them

—are presented to the Shah by Hoveyda. They need not be members of the *Majlis* but, with the creation of the Resurgence party, the Shah has decreed that they must all be party members. The Minister of the Interior, Jamshid Amuzgar, and Hushang Ansari, the Minister of Finance are thought to be the most influential of ministers. Of ever-increasing importance is PBO whose Director, Majid Majidi, was made a Minister of State in 1974. A new Minister, for Women's Affairs, Mrs Dowlatshahi, was appointed in 1976. A variety of activities are centred on the Prime Minister's office; here Hoveyda is assisted by a number of deputy prime ministers and special advisers, the latter being from time to time, of considerable importance. The growth in Government activity in recent years has obviously placed a great strain on all Government departments, particularly at the level of able chief executives and undersecretaries and the various ministries and departments. As the private sector has expanded and salaries have grown in response to market factors many government employees have seen their financial futures as lying outside the ministries.

The Ministry of the Interior is specifically responsible for the regional organisation which, since Darius's time, has been based on the governors general of large provinces. In a country the size of Iran these men have been of supreme importance in the past, frequently ruling as princes—known as *satraps*—which in years past, they in fact were. As Iran has developed there has been the usual tendency for all power to become centralised and, for a while, the provinces received insufficient attention and the governors general seemed to be diminishing in importance. This threat is now being reversed and far greater emphasis is being placed on regional development and greater administrative and financial powers are being given to the governors general to implement this.

The regional unit is the *ostan* of which there are now nineteen, together with three somewhat smaller areas, known as *farmandari-kols*. The *ostandar*, or governor general, is appointed by the Minister of Interior but is regarded as a specifically Shah appointment. Within each *ostan* there are a varying number of *shahrestans* (towns) each with its own governor; Khorasan has fifteen *shahrestans*, whilst Hamedan has only four. Each *shahrestan* is divided into *bakhsh* (district) and then further into *dehestans* (groups of villages). They are ruled over by *bakhshdars* and *dehdars* respectively.

An *ostandar* is an extremely important person, holding decentralised powers vested in him from the Monarch and Premier and being responsible for the implementation of Government policy within the *ostan*. Each government department has a sub-office within each *ostan*, where the chief executive is answerable both directly to Tehran and to the *ostandar*. As Hoveyda rules over his cabinet, so too does the *ostandar* over the regional sub-offices. Increasingly, *ostandars* are having wider powers of decision making and more funds at their discretion. An *ostandar* is head of the judiciary as well as the executive within his province. In the summer of 1975 *ostandars* were busy arresting, convicting and punishing local merchants for hoarding and excessive profiteering. Powerful themselves, they are also very vulnerable. It is not unknown for an *ostandar* to be removed at very short notice either as a result of his own ineptitude, or as a scapegoat, or because of a shift in the power structure in Tehran.

A foreigner wishing to understand Iran could hardly do better than spend a few minutes in an *ostandar*'s office. These offices are frequently large; invariably they are furnished with a vast desk complete with Iranian flags and portraits of the Shah, sometimes, too, of the royal family and Hoveyda, and with two rows of armchairs facing each other running at right angles to the desk. Opulence varies from the excessive to the spartan. Beautiful carpets are the rule; so too are air-conditioning, telephones and a continuous supply of cups of black tea and plates of biscuits. Business is done first-hand and comparatively little is committed to paper. The room invariably contains three or four people, frequently twenty or thirty. On arrival a visitor is extremely deferential, particularly the traditional villagers. A man's status is quickly shown by the reaction the visitor's greetings inspire in the *ostandar*. Once within the *ostandar*'s office, however, men speak their minds—often with passion. The 'phone rings virtually continuously. Sometimes it is Tehran sometimes a *farmandar*, frequently a local government official who has been summoned to explain an inefficiency. In the midst of all this an important visitor may arrive; the meetings cease forthwith, the crowd vanishes to an antechamber, all is peace and charm, fruit and nuts replace the biscuits and more tea arrives. The 'phone shatters the peace . . . 'The Prime Minister's office wants to know . . .', and so it continues. A veritable nightmare for the uninitiated, a maelstrom for the conventional, but a scheme which works despite all its faults. In an *ostandar*'s office, as in so many other places in Iran, it is not what, but who you know that matters.

Of increasing importance in each *ostan* is the regional branch of PBO where the local development plans are being formulated and where are to be found the brightest of the government employees. With increasing funds allocated for regional development, particularly the building up of a regional infrastructure of roads, services and government buildings to enable this to take place, the recommendations of this office are obviously important and local interests are represented to it with fervour. Such decentralisation of real authority is something which will take time for Iranian society to appreciate, a society which, in the past, has had no such responsibility. But it is important to the wellbeing of the provinces and to the growth of a responsible society that this should be encouraged.

THE JUDICIARY

The Iranian judicial system is based on the French pattern produced by Adolphe Perni in 1911 but a commission was established in December 1974 to enquire into the possibility of adapting certain aspects of the British-based Anglo-Saxon system. This would, amongst other things, probably involve the British principle that the accused is innocent until proved guilty. The Ministry of Justice, in announcing this commission, said that it was hoped that a way could be found of speeding up legal proceedings. That the system is not working well and that the Shah is impatient with it was shown by a recent statement: 'It is not justice to have the guilty at large in the streets. Yet precious few have been the occasions when I have seen the corrupt and guilty condemned and duly punished by the Ministry of Justice. It is especially in this direction that I should like to see more dynamism in the Iranian judicial system.'

It seems hard to understand how a really equitable legal system can exist when the *Savak* courts operate in the way they do. Within these courts only *Savak* statements are accepted and there is no cross-questioning of witnesses by the defendant or his counsel. The cases are heard in secret. Very few acquittals have been made following such military tribunals. However, there have been a number of amnesties heard recently; 1,200 were granted in the year 1975–6 with a further 451 amnesties granted to people convicted by military tribunals on the occasion of the Shah's birthday in October 1976. However, Iran has signed the Universal Declaration of Human Rights and the Shah does speak strongly in favour of the principles contained therein. Recently, a campaign against profiteering has seen many well-to-do Iranians arrested, the mayor of Isfahan exiled to the Afghan border, the chief executive of the Isfahan Sugar Company imprisoned and the one-time head of the Navy fined \$3·7 million and imprisoned for five years for embezzlement. In May 1976 the officials of the Abbasabad reconstruction project were charged by the Supreme Court with having accepted bribes totalling R15 million (\$200,000). A number of cases of bribery by international companies in order to gain contracts have been unearthed and the recipients harshly punished. 'Respect our laws' Hoveyda told the US Financial Conference held in Tehran in March 1976. 'Along with goods and services, it appears we have imported a business morality which is more accurately a lack of morality.' But it is hard to expect such an attitude to bribery to change too quickly in a land where *bakshish* (tipping) has been so well established.

TAXATION

Non-oil revenues contributed only 13·6 per cent to the Iranian Government revenue in the year 1974–5 which was almost evenly balanced between direct and indirect taxation, to yield R157,932 million. This represented a 40 per cent growth in direct taxation collected over the previous year, but only 2 per cent on indirect taxation.

Income tax is, by current Western standards, delightfully low. Employees in the private sector have paid income tax at the following rates since August 1974:

Up to 12,000 rials a month—no tax. Approximately £1,200 a year
Between 12,000 rials and 20,000—8 per cent on that in excess of 12,000 rials
Between 20,000 rials and 34,000—10 per cent on that in excess of 20,000 rials
Between 34,000 rials and 60,000—12 per cent on that in excess of 34,000 rials

For example, a man earning R60,000 a month, which is roughly equivalent to £6,000 a year, would pay approximately £500 tax. In the United Kingdom this would be more likely to be £2,000. The situation is even more attractive for Government employees who pay tax at a still lower rate, as well as lower rates for employees of government companies. Collection of taxes which, in the past, has been notoriously inefficient is now subject to far tighter and fairer controls.

However, the Minister of Economy and Finance, Ansari, warned at a Conference in Bandar Pahlavi in 1975 that such taxation must rise, on the Shah's instructions, to 50 per cent of the revenue within ten years so that Iran will be able to maintain its economic development when the oil revenues begin to fall. Iranians, nevertheless, regard this as being in the very long-term future and currently enjoy salaries but little depleted by the Inland Revenue. At the same conference Ansari complained that, of 20,000 companies registered in Tehran, only 9,362 had any tax records and only 5,493 submitted a tax return for the previous year. A sample of those who did make a return, however, showed that 43 per cent claimed to be running at a loss, 3 per cent breaking even and only 53 per cent making a profit. 'Such figures do not agree with the country's economic boom', Ansari noted. Improved book-keeping, one imagines, will soon be implemented.

5

How They Live

MOST Iranians still live in the country and most of their houses are still built, in the conventional way, from mud bricks. Only the minority of houses have piped water, though those with electricity are now in the majority. Sewage systems are, generally, still a dream.

This does not coincide with the image that Iran would like to project to the outside world and is something which urban Iranians will hardly trouble to think about; it is, nevertheless, well understood by the Shah and his planners. There has not been an even spread of the new wealth and the gap between urban and rural development has been seen to widen in the last decade. Agriculture, obviously the mainstay of rural life, has for long been the Cinderella of the Iranian economy.

Iran's population has increased fourfold since Reza Shah came to the throne: in 1921 the population was about 8 million while in late 1976 it was approaching 35 million and still growing at 3·2 per cent per annum. With the intention of limiting this population growth, a birth control programme was launched in 1967 with the intention of cutting the growth rate to 1·5 per cent. If this is achieved a population of 49 million could be expected by the end of the century while, if the present rate is maintained, the population by then would exceed 70 million. At the start of the Pahlavi era, 79 per cent of the population, or 6·4 million people, lived outside the towns; the percentage has now fallen to 60 per cent but the actual number of people has increased to 21 million.

Rural population in Iran is essentially nucleated—very few

people live away from the villages and small towns. The reasons for this are easily appreciated. Water is a scarce commodity over the majority of the country so that settlement is clustered wherever this is available, be it an open stream, a spring or wherever the enterprise of a landlord has provided a *qanat*. In a country where law and order was notoriously ineffective it was a foolish family who lived away from the protection of their colleagues. Consequently, villages grew, not just because of the availability of water, but as defensive sites giving protection against stray bandits and, in troubled times, small armies of dissident tribesfolk. The walls that were built for protection still stand, though in most cases the villages have outgrown them and new houses have been built with no thought of defence except perhaps against marauding wolves in the more remote of the mountain areas. The gates have been torn down and the gateways widened to allow the ubiquitous lorry to get into the village to load and unload its wares.

There are thought to be some 50,000 villages—though some politicians place the number as high as 60,000. To the officials of PBO the task of raising the standard of living of these villages is daunting. The average size of a village—about 500 people— and their frequent remoteness, makes the cost of providing even basic essentials almost prohibitive. Yet, in the past twelve years great changes have occurred and most of these became apparent before the riches of the oil revenues became available. The work of the Literacy Corps, Medical Corps and the Agricultural Advisers will be discussed later but it was these units of the White Revolution that reached into the smallest villages and stirred the traditional inertia in such a way that it is now the villagers themselves who are generating change.

Water supplies and population growth and decline are intrinsically connected. The traveller in Iran may be excused if he makes the common mistake of assuming that the vast number of ruined settlements that litter the country bespeak a once far greater population. That the population has fluctuated is undoubted but the ruins are those of abandoned settlements frequently caused by either the drying up of springs or the silting up of the *qanats*, so encouraging their inhabitants to move elsewhere. We know little about population numbers in previous centuries though we can be sure that the fifty million quoted for the time of Darius or the forty million given by Chardin for the height of the Safavid dynasty in the seventeenth century are wildly inaccurate. Reasonable authenticity can be given to the estimate of ten million for 1850, a figure reduced to six million by cholera and famine by 1873. Insufficient water has led to frequent famines while poisoned water has been responsible for innumerable epidemics of cholera in previous centuries. The present population explosion can be correlated not only with better food and medicines but with piped water supplies and a control of sewage.

While the majority of the population still live in villages, it is urban Iran with which the visitor will first become acquainted —indeed most visitors, to their own disadvantage, get little further than the so-called oriental styled bars of the large international hotels. Urban Iran is flourishing and is growing at a faster rate than the country as a whole as rural migrants swell the already virile population. Most Iranian cities appear essentially modern and it is hard to realise that the country has urban traditions as ancient as any—indeed, in years to come, when archaeologists have studied just some of the myriad ruins, the Iranian plateau could well boast the sites of the world's most ancient cities. Ecbatana was the summer capital of Xerxes in the fifth century BC while modern Damghan has been suggested as the ancient Hekatompylos, or City of the Hundred Gates, a name given it by the Greeks when it was the capital of the Arsacid dynasty of the Parthian kings. Susa, too, was a major city figuring in Old Testament times. Until recently, however, the cities have remained small, and the exception, on the Iranian landscape.

Now mainly of nostalgic interest, but until very recently of considerable political importance, are the tribes of Iran and their essentially nomadic existence. At the turn of the century perhaps a quarter of the population was in some way nomadic but now the numbers have been reduced to some half a million persons whose entire lives are dominated by the twice-yearly migrations. Chief amongst these are the Bakhtiari and the Quashqai tribes whose winter quarters are on the coastal plain fringing the Gulf but whose summer pastures are high in the Zagros Mountains. They are essentially pasturalists and it is the need for fresh grass for their considerable herds that governs the pattern of their annual migrations. Curzon wrote:

> *The physical conformation of Persia, presenting as it does the extreme vicissitudes of climate, corresponding with those of altitude, from the enervating heat of the coastal plains to the rigours of mountain heights rarely left by the snow; the racial features and archaic habits of many of its peoples; and the unsettled character of its government, are responsible for a phenomenon that has almost disappeared from the organisation of other states upon which civilisation had in any degree laid its crystallising finger . . .*
>
> *In Persia, on the other hand, where population is sparse, where the cultivatable area is relatively small, and where great spaces are occupied by bleak mountain districts, remote from the control of government, and adapted to pastoral rather than agricultural pursuits, the immemorial prescription of the East still survives; the tribes move in compact detachments according to the period of the year, carrying with them their entire household furniture and wealth, and exchanging the lowland valleys or riverain plains, which they have occupied during the winter, for the higher and cooler crests, where life is supportable in the summer heat.*

So it was in 1892, and could well have been one, two or three thousand years earlier. That such an adaptation to the physical environment is probably now passing merits more consideration than the numbers remaining might seem to justify.

The tribes were, and to an extent still are, highly organised and disciplined units owing unfailing loyalty to their chieftain, or *khan*, whose authority was devolved through each head of family down to each tent. It was feudal; it was patriarchal. 'My authority must not be contested or discussed. Should I feel that among all my men five only were against me I would abdicate without delay', said a Quashqai *khan* in the 1960s. No land was held individually but all in common. Group loyalty was paramount, so too was hospitality to strangers. 'They are hospitable, domestic, simple-minded, innocent of the foul debaucheries of the city Persian. On the other hand, they are rough, ignorant and sometimes fierce, they glory in plunder, and are, in many cases, adroit thieves. Little practical religion is known to them but that of blood, which vents itself in family feuds, pursued with unslaked ferocity till whole households have sometimes been extirpated . . .' (Curzon). On being shown the city of Calcutta, a chieftain exclaimed, 'What a noble place to plunder!' Whilst another chieftain, questioning Beg Jan of Bokhara about the nature of paradise, asked if there was any raiding to be had there. On hearing that there was not he exclaimed, 'Ah, then Paradise won't do for me!'

Successive dynasties have feared the powers of the tribes not least, perhaps, because practically every Persian dynasty was founded, at least initially, on tribal powers. Reza Shah himself certainly feared the tribes as a threat to his own sovereignty but he also thought of them, quite genuinely, as being an anachronism and therefore, like the *chardor* (the black robe worn by Moslem women, often used to mask their faces), as something which had to be abolished. His policy involved both the breaking of the *khan*'s authority and enforced settlement of the tribes. Many of the tribal chieftains were imprisoned, executed or exiled. The campaigns were carried out with great ferocity on both sides but it must not be forgotten that, in these campaigns, Reza Shah was fighting for his own existence as a political leader and was regarded by the tough aristocratic tribal *khans* as an upstart usurper. As each *khan* was deposed military officers were placed in charge of the tribes and given specific instructions to enforce sedentarisation. Tribal life suffered immediately. Sheep and goats perished in vast numbers as they failed to find the grass in one place that they had previously found in many pastures on their annual migrations. Disease spread amongst the tribesmen whose way of life depended on constant movement to remove the threats from inadequate hygiene.

Eventually, the tribes were allowed to migrate again but only because of the meat shortage that Reza Shah's policy had created. Migrations continued after his abdication but it had been sufficiently demonstrated that the independence of the *khan* relied on the authority of the Shah so that tribal life never returned to its original level. The implementation of land reform in 1963 led to the last confrontation between the tribal *khans* and central government. Seeing land reform as being a further threat to their nomadic way of life, as well as to their wealth, a number of the tribes openly rebelled; they were no match for modern warfare and were defeated. The Shah, pursuing a wiser and more liberal policy than had his father, then sought by economic considerations to encourage sedentarisation. While the tribes are free to migrate, and some half a million still do so, the alternatives are being made even more attractive. Well planned towns and villages are being established in tribal country and every facility is being put at the disposal of the tribesman who wishes to settle. The harshness of nomadic life is now becoming the more obvious as a result of these contrasts. High in the Zagros Mountains, the Bazuft River presents the greatest challenge in the twice-yearly migration of the Bakhtiari tribe. The fit and active, both human and animal, find no difficulty in crossing. But for the old it is an ever-increasing worry. Each crossing sees some of the older sheep swept away to their death by the river's strong currents, while the oldest and most infirm people know that they too, one day, will either fail to make the crossing or will accept the inevitable and remain behind to die as the tribe crosses over. Such an old age does not appeal to the young, who know more and more of the alternatives.

Paradoxically, there is now a change in government policy, if not as dramatic as it is emotional, in favour of the tribal life. Tribal costumes and the nomadic existence is what the tourist wants to see and tourism is an increasing trade. But the rugged tribesmen of previous decades would have scorned an American's or a German's camera and those tribesmen who now perform in cabaret and the hotels probably do not know the rigours of crossing the Bazuft River. And Iran is now experiencing another meat shortage—and is importing mutton from New Zealand.

If the day of the nomad is now almost over, the progression from a pastoral nomadic to a settled semi-pastoral, semi-arable existence has been a feature of Iranian life for centuries. A wealthy tribal *khan* would frequently purchase land away from the tribal pastures and arrange for some of his tribesfolk to settle; it was, after all, the only way to remove the pressure on grazing grounds if the population of the tribe grew too large. The tribes, though nomadic, practised arable farming. Grain was planted in the spring as the tribes moved up into the mountains and harvested on the tribes' autumn migrations to winter grazing grounds.

On the edge of tribal country, particularly in the Zagros foothills, the villages are, in some ways, only semi-settled. In summer many of the people leave their houses and take to the hills with their black tents and herds and remain away for months on end. Others leave the villages in summer for temporary work on construction sites or in the cities, returning only when the weather closes in on the project, or when the crops must be harvested in the village. Strong similarities can be seen here both with the shielings of the crofters of north-west Scotland and the seasonal labour from the *gaeltacht* of Ireland.

Iranian villages appear to lack any conscious plan and seem to resemble an historical accident or series of adaptations. Frequently, villages are sited on the sides of hills where the flat roof of one house is in juxtaposition to the wall of the next. Roads, as such, within villages are, if they exist at all, an accident and may well double as the river. Most pathways are narrow, tortuous, unsurfaced and, to the Western mind, unhygienic. Invariably, the building material is sunbaked brick covered with a veneer of plastered mud. Roofs are invariably flat and made out of poplar trunks laid parallel and covered with brushwood and then more mud. Obviously, individual building styles vary across such a vast country, but the groupings of rooms around a central courtyard is practically universal. The majority of structures are single-storied with the exception of the main apartments approached by steps from the courtyard to a balcony off which open two or sometimes three rooms. Within the compound are store rooms, bakery, kitchen and in some instances rooms in which the looms are set up for the making of carpets. A single entrance, closed and bolted at night, gives on to the 'street'. In all too many Iranian homes water still arrives in open ditches flowing through the yard and into this selfsame ditch passes the family waste—only to be delivered to the next house. Thankfully, water schemes now give standpipes in most villages and drinking water is carried in buckets. But washing, and sometimes cooking, is done with water from the ditch—the toilet facilities are best passed over! But home for the villager is, nevertheless, not without its comforts. Even the poorest keep their living spaces clean and cover the floor with home-made rugs while the homes of the wealthier villagers contain many rugs laid on top of each other that would command a high price in a Western store. Rugs are the main item of furniture and double as chairs and beds as well. During the day pillows and blankets are kept piled to one side. Tin trunks, often of elaborate design, contain the family valuables. Rifles are hung on the wall. Niches, formed in the mud-plaster walls, will contain knick-knacks, radio sets and oil lanterns, if electricity has not as yet been made available. Few homes would be without a picture of the Shah and, increasingly, the Crown Prince. Frequently in the same frame will be a picture of the prophet Ali and in a number of homes a trinity is made with a picture of the Virgin Mary holding the baby Jesus—a reassurance, perhaps, of the role of women which Islam has been slow to reveal to its adherents.

Shoes are left at the door and the visitor will sit cross-legged on the carpet while being entertained by the host. The inevitable tea will be served from the ever-hot samovar, prepared by the women of the family who, even now in the villages, will remain in a subservient and retiring position, at least when there are visitors. Iranian hospitality is best experienced in such village homes as these.

If the administrative reforms inspired by the White Revolution of 1963 have so far made only superficial changes to the visual aspect of Iranian villages, far greater changes are on their way. Already government agencies are building schools, clinics, dispensaries, gendarme posts and the like in an architectural style that is, almost apologetically, deferential to eastern tradition. Undoubtedly, the proposals for agricultural development being fostered by the current five-year plan will change the village scene dramatically in the next few years.

URBAN IRAN—TEHRAN

'The first appearance of Tehran is agreeable after a long journey, but in no sense imposing', wrote Curzon. 'It was difficult to believe that the green band could shroud a great city of nearly 200,000 souls. The only building that rose to any height above the level of the treetops appeared to be a large mosque, with four tiled minarets . . .' Since Curzon's time in Iran this agreeable, if unimposing city has grown to be one of the foremost cities of the world, with a population of some $4\frac{1}{2}$ million and a growth rate of $6\frac{1}{2}$ per cent per annum; even its greatest advocates could never claim it to be much other than brash.

Tehran, whilst being the capital and largest city in the country, is in a class of its own; Isfahan and Mashad are major cities but they still retain a greater vestige of the East than does Tehran. The growth of the city has been rapid. As recently as 1925 the city gates were locked at night; now all traces of the walls have gone and the city sprawls in all directions though least, perhaps, towards Shemiran, the exclusive residential area to the north. Land prices in the city centre have risen astronomically. Almost all buildings before the 1950s have been torn down along the main boulevards and have been replaced by endless glass, steel and concrete structures of an indifferent international design. At no time has this process been more rapid than it is at present as international companies compete with each other for prestigious office accommodation and government departments proliferate in a desperate bid to keep abreast of economic advance. The walled compounds of the British and Russian embassies off Ferdowsi introduce a much-needed relief of greenery into a central area of tarmac and concrete, as well as providing a glimpse of what an older Tehran might have been. Hotels belonging to international chains have blossomed like so many forced plants, as they compete for the trade of the wealthy. Within a short while of opening, the Royal Tehran Hilton had built a twin tower block. An even larger hotel than the Hilton—the Intercontinental, or Sheraton—is now being built by the Japanese, thirty storeys in height with 704 rooms, while the older hotels like the Park or the Mar Mar seem somewhat aghast at the speed with which they have been overtaken.

Traditionally, Tehrani society has been classified by how far 'up the hill' it can afford to live. That area around the railway station and the bazaar is insufferably hot in summer while land prices 500 metres higher in Shemiran and Tajrash are so exorbitant that none but the very rich can contemplate owning or renting an apartment, let alone a house, in that area which can just detect a slight breeze on a summer's evening.

In 1975 the Iranian Problems Study Group reported:

> *Tehran has so many problems that it could never hope to become a metropolis in the known sense of the word at least for the next 25 years . . . Tehran has no discipline nor any established criteria. Its administration is uncertain; the local municipality, the town council and even the city council play no part in its administration . . . co-operation from the citizenry is negligible.*

The growth in the city's population has resulted from the large influx from other cities, so that only just over half the population are Tehrani by birth. Housing is a major problem. The new migrants tend to settle in the older, cheaper areas of south Tehran in what is already a desperately over-crowded area. Currently, the Government is involved in major slum

F

clearing schemes, one of which involves the building of a new satellite overspill at Shush to provide 14,000 apartments. A further 13,000 such apartments are being built to the east of Shahrzad Avenue and will be completed late in 1976.

While the plight of slum dwellers in south Tehran is grim, that for higher income groups is little better in a city where, as yet, very little Government or local authority building is taking place. With demand always outstripping supply, the rate for apartments has risen dramatically—it is not uncommon for a two bedroom apartment in a moderately acceptable area of the city to cost £250 a month, and the average monthly rate for an apartment was given as $254 in 1976.

Increasing affluence is likely to reduce Tehran to a standstill by 1984, according to one recent estimate. In 1970 there were just over 300,000 vehicles in the city, in 1974 it was 800,00 and since then it has increased at a rate of 300 a day. Tehran was never built for this. The road system is essentially that of a grid iron and, for all the building of the Shahyad expressways, route ways, over- and under-passes, etc, the city will never be able to cope. The average speed of a city bus—for what this might mean—has fallen from 24km per hour in 1956 to 14 in 1965 and 7 in 1974, whilst even the taxis can average only 14km per hour in downtown Tehran! After who-knows-what effort, a further statistic has been produced—Tehranis spend 2 million hours a day waiting behind red traffic lights, queuing for buses or waiting for taxis!

For long years the enthusiast has pinned his hopes on a metro system. Many plans have been produced, revised, discarded, redrawn. In March 1976 it was finally announced that agreement had been reached with the Paris Authority for Public Transport (RATP) for feasibility studies to be completed within twenty months and for work to then start on the building of a 63km network comprising four lines; the project is estimated at R90 billion and will take nine years to complete. By then, perhaps, Tehranis will have been forced to abandon their cars and will have become accustomed to walking.

The future looks grim. At the International Union of Local

Authorities held in Tehran in 1975 it was stated that the planned expansion of the city was for 5·5 million people in 1990 but that unless stringent measures are taken the figure could be reached within four years—without any marked outward expansion of the city. If the original master plan were followed, the delegates were told, Tehran could reach 16–20 million by 1990.

Even now, however, there are places within which to escape in Tehran. It costs nothing to walk through the old covered bazaar, the biggest in the East, and discuss the price of carpets for hours on end with dealers whose shrewdness is matched by the knowledge that carpet prices are rising by some 35 per cent a year and will continue to climb even more rapidly as supplies dwindle. It costs very little to look, or perhaps to gawp, at the Crown Jewels, the world's most fantastic collection of precious stones, whose value underwrites three-quarters of the nation's currency. For nothing you can see the Zurkhaneh (House of Strength) and, if you are lucky, find a seat in a park. If you can afford it you can eat well but you will find it difficult to relax, at almost any price, and so, like all true Tehranis, the visitor to Iran will look to the other cities of the country.

ISFAHAN

Isfahan is the second city of Iran. 'In Isfahan', writes Blunt, 'the balance between East and West is still delicately maintained'. Using the wealth that was rapidly accumulating to the country as European traders sought the riches of the East, Shah Abbas built the fabled city that was to become the home of Haji Baba and of which sufficient remains to give credence to the claim that 'Isfahan is half the world'. In the great Maidan with the Ali Qapu palace to the right, the Lutfullah Mosque to the left and the splendid dome and twin minarets of the Royal Shah Mosque rising in front against the deep blue of the skies, no visitor can fail to feel transported to another era and clime. The Isfahani feels this and is proud. Modern Isfahan cherishes its heritage and is aware of its economic potential for tourism.

Despite the sacking of the city in 1720 by the Afghans who then built a triumphal mound of 70,000 human skulls, there remains sufficient to make Isfahan the prime tourist centre of the country. The world's most exotic hotel must surely be the Shah Abbas, sometimes requisitioned by the Shah when he is in Isfahan. Other hotels for more humble needs are being built, giving a range of service to suit all tastes.

Isfahan is now an industrial city where the factory hooter is louder than the muezzin's call. Chardin, writing in the seventeenth century, spoke of the industrial wealth of the city, while Curzon, with a blast of colonial pride, wrote of the bazaar:

> *The English eye is gratified by the sight of English trade marks on nine out of every ten bales of merchandise that pass on camel, donkey or mule; and enquiry elicits the satisfactory fact that Manchester is still the universal clothier of Isfahan . . .*

Not so now. Isfahan is a major textile centre in its own right and the Shahnaz mills are the largest in Iran. A revival in craft industry in the 1920s has been maintained, despite difficulties, and the finest quality carpets, textiles, ceramics and silverware are made within the city. Sugar mills and cement plants contribute greatly to the city's industrial wealth.

By far the most significant development, however, has been the building of the steel mill at Aryamehr, built by the Russians in the famous 'Gas for Steel Deal' in 1965 and which came on stream in March 1973. As the mill was being built the expectation of its capacity was always being revised—upwards! Designed to produce 600,000 tons per annum in 1973 and 1·9 million tons in 1978, plans were announced in 1975 to increase capacity to 4 million tons by 1980 and 6 million in 1983. Such industrial activity has led to major housing problems and it was estimated that some 30 per cent of the city's population were living in properties that were either unhygienic or unsafe— the number constantly increasing due to a 12 per cent growth rate. A satellite town, Aryashahr, is being built a few kilometres away from the steel mills with a scheduled population of

300,000. The Isfahani has a reputation for industry as well as for a certain Scottish cannyness which could well help to restore this once proud, and now rich and still beautiful, city to national prominence.

OTHER CITIES

Whilst Tehran stands in a class of its own there are other cities which resemble Isfahan: Mashad is distinctly more oriental, while Tabriz, which is slightly smaller, has had an even longer connection with Europe through the trading activities of the Armenians. Shiraz is a more flamboyant version of Isfahan some 400km further to the south, the home of Hafez and Saadi and beautiful roses. Abadan, Ahvaz and Khorramshahr, numbering together some three-quarters of a million people, are the centres of the oil and associated industries and the port developments of Khuzistan. Kermanshah, Rezaiyeh, Hamedan, Kerman, Ardebil, Yazd are regional centres of varying sizes and importance. All are essentially old, well established cities which have seen developments either to a larger, or a very large, extent in recent years. Hamedan is probably the oldest and, due to excessive road building in the 1970s, has perhaps changed most.

Semnan might be regarded as typical of the smaller regional centres. Situated 300km east of Tehran on the edge of the Kavir it has been an important route centre for centuries. The Golden Road to Samarkand passed here, as did travellers like Marco Polo and pillagers like Genghiz Khan and the Afghans. The railway was built in the 1930s but the road has been kept unsurfaced in an attempt to keep, one suspects, the pilgrim traffic on the railway. It has a population of 45,000, representing a 50 per cent increase in 10 years, which is in keeping with urban growth. The city is well wooded with trees and irrigation ditches lining most streets. The centre is dominated by the Islamic trilogy of mosque, bazaar and bath house where the latter two finance the former. All are in active use, well cared for and appear unaware of the antics of tourists. Curzon says: 'Semnan is held remarkable in Persia for its extensive and well irrigated gardens, for its ancient trees, for an old minaret . . . for a smart and well-preserved modern mosque, for its local manufactures of teacakes and blue cotton pyjamas, for the beauty of its women, and for the unintelligibility of its speech.' Curzon felt it did not 'quite answer to expectations' but was well worth inspecting. The modern housing outside the town is pleasing and unpretentious, the *Qajar* gateway bespeaks an earlier opulence but the governor-general's office which, as late as 1971, was made of mud brick is now a marble faced structure with fitted carpets within and fountains without. It is a quiet city, where tea is still drunk at leisure in pleasant *chaikhanehs*, where the traffic is slow and wealth seems as much based on locally-produced tobacco as it does on government-financed developments. It is too near Tehran to have grown large, and not far enough away to have received an embarrassment of government largess.

THE CONSUMER SOCIETY

Urbanisation and the consumer society have developed simultaneously. Truly, one may see tribesfolk carrying transistor radios and serving iced drinks out of vacuum flasks, but it is in the cities that the full effects of the consumer society are to be seen. In the twelve years following the 1963 Revolution the growth in consumer good purchases was prodigious; in 1963 there had been sold 1,300 TV sets and 6,000 refrigerators but, twelve years later, the annual sale of TV sets and refrigerators both passed the half million mark with 90 per cent of each being produced in Iran. The sale of telephones rose from 30,000 to 300,000, and of cars from 11,000 to 142,000 during the same period.

The domestic market is fed by 6,000 factories and a quarter of a million workshops but is now supplemented by billions of dollars worth of imports. The road from Europe, reaching Iran at the border post of Bazargun, sees a constant stream of juggernauts—85,000 in 1975—carrying smoked salmon and hi-fi equipment, textiles, shoes, machinery and anything else that the wit of man can devise and sell. Whole new professions have been established in a short time: advertising executives, marketing and research specialists, retailing experts, distribution advisers and the like. The rate of increase in consumer demand during the early 1970s was steady at 18 per cent per annum, but, in 1975, it climbed to still higher levels.

Iranians are better fed than at any time in the past. The consumption of vegetable shortening has increased fourfold since 1963, sugar consumption eightfold and the consumption of soft drinks by a staggering thirteenfold. The overall daily intake of calories which was 1,600 in 1948–9, 2,030 in 1964–5 reached 2,400 in 1974–5, the World Health Organisation recommended minimum standard being 2,700. The consumption of protein has risen from 47g in 1948–9 to 70g in 1974–5. Of course, the quality of food varies immensely across the country with twice as many calories being consumed in rural Kermanshah as in urban Kerman. The consumption of more calories within the country districts is a universal phenomenon. Meat consumption is rising rapidly with a spectacular 23 per cent rise in one year in Tehran. However, at only 18kg of red meat per capita annually it could take many years for supplies to be sufficiently organised so that consumption reached European, let alone American, levels.

Eating habits are changing rapidly. The traditional staple has been rice, bread and tea with mutton, goat, chicken, vegetables and fruit added as income has allowed. For millions of Iranians a breakfast of tea—black, with sugar—and bread remains the traditional start to the day. A cooked meal comprising large quantities, at least by European standards, of rice served with either grilled or stewed meat or fowl is deemed necessary at some stage of the day, normally during the early afternoon. Bowls of *mast*, a thick yogurt with a very rich skin, and jugs of *dogh*, a watered down yogurt marinated with herbs, are served at all times. Goats' and sheeps' milk, cheese, eggs either boiled, fried or as omelettes, and vegetables are extras to any meal.

Potatoes are normally expensive and treated as a delicacy Tomatoes—*goojeh-ferangee* in Farsi—which literally translated means 'food of the foreigner' are very popular, as are cucumbers and onions. Fruit is served almost everywhere; melons seem always to be in season while apples, pears, peaches, cherries and grapes add pleasing and succulent variety. Nuts, especially the pistachio, are found everywhere. Spices are not commonly used.

Traditionally, Iranian cooking has been based on boiling and grilling, with the oven reserved only for the baking of bread —a function that the Persian oven is probably best adjusted to perform. With increasing affluence more and more Iranians are using European styled ovens, pressure cookers, refrigerators and deep freezes and there has been a corresponding increase in the range and quality of food that is served. Within the home, however, most food is still traditional in form but served in greater quantity and of better quality than before.

The rapid growth in both affluence and population numbers, linked to world shortages of basic foodstuffs, led to a great increase in their price during the summer of 1975. Many traders hoarded supplies and prices, it appeared, went up far higher than was necessary. The government took swift action. Traders who charged disproportionately high prices were jailed and their goods seized. $300 million were spent on temporary subsidies to cushion the housewife against the shock of rising prices.

The range of food available, at least in Tehran and in some of the more favoured localities of the larger cities, is impressive —so, too, is the price. Delicacies from Paris, London and the United States, as well as the humble Mallaig kipper, can all be found in the increasingly popular supermarkets. For most Iranians, however, shopping is still conventional. Fruit and general groceries come from the bazaar, or local shop, bread from the bakery and meat from a butcher. Cleanliness is improving. The use of refrigerators has led to an increase in pre-packaged foods. Milk is more freely available and is issued to all schoolchildren.

Beer is brewed in Tehran and a number of other centres and is freely available in most urban areas, even on draught. To expatriates it lacks the taste of 'the real thing', and visions of Olde English pubs serving pints of proprietary beers are the subject of much affectionate reminiscence on hot summer days. Vodka is made in Iran and, though considerably more expensive than it was, is still comparatively cheap. Whisky—the real thing and in a pleasing variety of types—is available but at three or four times the price in Britain. The best hotels and restaurants sell European wines, but seldom good vintages, even though the price is exorbitant; Iranian wine, however, can be good when found. It should, however, be remembered that Iran is a Moslem country and the drinking of alcohol, while now reasonably common, is still not publicly acceptable in the more traditional areas.

Iranians have become far more clothes conscious with increasing affluence, with Tehranis anxiously watching, and responding to, the latest changes in international fashion. The provinces are prepared, it seems, to watch and speculate on this aspect of Western culture while the country districts remain unaware of all the fuss.

The *chardor*, despite having been banned by the Reza Shah, is still worn because it is coolest and most convenient in hot and dusty weather but, as often as not, a miniskirt or thigh-clinging jeans will be glimpsed beneath. In country districts women will still be found wearing colourful tribal skirts and shawls while the men wear baggy trousers and loose-fitting shirts. The transition from this to more conventional Western wear for men is straightforward. The trousers become less baggy, the shirts have a better cut and jackets appear. For women the change seems to take place beneath the *chardor* and, like a chrysalis, a modern woman may appear even in a nomadic encampment.

Outside the cities, home-produced clothes or those purchased in the bazaars are the rule. Shoes are of poor quality and are frequently, particularly for children, made of plastic. Suits for men are made by streetside tailors. Freshly ironed and starched shirts, a status symbol anywhere, are the raison d'être of the endless steam laundries to be found in any back street.

Tehran has no large departmental stores nor clothing stores of a size comparable to a Western capital, but it does have an increasing number of small, chic and fashion-conscious clothes shops where prices are very high and, one suspects, profit margins are immense. Although women are fully emancipated at law Iranian husbands have a more traditional view of a woman's role than many of their wives would wish. For a wife to work is seen, by many an Iranian man, as an insult to his ability to support her. Bored wives are to be found in numbers in such shops frittering away their husbands' money on clothes of doubtful quality and indifferent cut. Yearly, or twice-yearly pilgrimages are made to those larger emporia on the Champs-Elysées, Fifth Avenue or Knightsbridge. The names of Harrods and Marks and Spencers are often alluded to by the wealthy but, it would all too often seem, indiscriminating purchasers. Large sums of money are spent, but too much is taken without payment. Is it the need for excitement (it cannot be the lack of money) that causes far too many Iranian shoplifters to appear before the magistrates with several hundred pounds worth of unpaid-for merchandise?

Iranians also leave their country if they need, or think they need, advanced medical care. The London Clinic is a status symbol in a way that no Tehran hospital could hope to emulate. In earlier years Iranians would have been well justified in turning to London and elsewhere for medical attention but conditions have changed quickly and the standard of medicine in the best Tehran hospitals is now high.

There are some 11,000 doctors and 1,500 dentists in Iran, giving a ratio of one doctor to 3,000 patients and a dentist to every 20,000. High ratios, indeed, but when the predominance of Tehran is noticed, the situation is even worse. Nearly half the doctors practise in the capital (1:789); 3,000 more work in other urban areas, giving just 2,000 doctors to serve the rural population of 21 million. The situation of the dentists is even more alarming; half of these are in Tehran, leaving a mere 700 over the rest of the country. Even though Tehran is an attractive place for the medical profession to practise, the country as a whole has suffered badly from the 'brain drain'. In the past forty years some 12,000 Iranians have graduated from medical schools within Iran and roughly the same number from foreign medical faculties. Of this 24,000 some are obviously dead, retired or have given up medicine, but that still leaves very large numbers currently working abroad. It is thought that some 3,500 Iranian doctors are practising in Germany while 300 Iranian doctors a year are accepted by the US. By 1970 90 per cent of the medical graduates of Pahlavi University in Shiraz and 40 per cent of those from Tehran University were going to the US. This has represented a terrific drain on Iranian resources and while many valid reasons—better pay, social conditions, professional conditions as well as worries about national service and paperwork—have been given, it is not the vote of confidence from the professional people that the country needs and it has given the medical profession a bad public image. To combat this, new legislation introduced in 1976 will offer grants for university courses only to those students who will undertake to work in the country for a minimum number of years after graduation.

In late 1975 it was estimated that 3,500 Indian, Filipino and South Korean doctors would have been recruited to work in Iran leaving, one is faced to wonder, just what ratios of patients to doctors in their own countries? Meanwhile a special committee is touring the US endeavouring to persuade doctors to return to their homeland. What price Hippocrates?

The building of hospitals has proceeded apace. Between 1963 and 1975 the number of hospitals increased from 352 to 550 and the number of beds from 24,000 to 45,000. Clinics have increased from 1,500 to 2,800. A further 20,000 beds are projected for completion by 1978. Obviously, most Iranian hospitals are modern; they are also well equipped. Within Tehran the standard of medical care can be very high and the equipment is amongst some of the most sophisticated in the world. Outside the capital the woeful shortage of nurses as well as doctors severely limits their effectiveness.

Despite the difficulties, the medical service has achieved a great deal in recent years. Many diseases have been reduced or eradicated. Malaria is now almost unknown; so is tuberculosis. Trachoma which once led to blindness for thousands of desert dwellers has now been brought under control. Cholera outbreaks are speedily contained. A nationwide vaccination programme started in 1974 to protect the population from such diseases as smallpox, measles, diphtheria and others. Infant mortality has fallen to 110 per 1,000 births. Life expectancy which, in 1963 was forty-one, is now fifty-three. Expenditure on all levels of medicine doubled in the two years 1974–6. Some of this, no doubt, is accounted for by the widespread use of tranquillisers, which seems to have become a feature of certain lifestyles in Tehran.

Medical insurance and pension schemes are still in their infancy. Within government service and certain of the major industries—the oil industry being a pace-setter—pensions and insurance are provided, the payments being linked to years of service. In 1974 the Shah stated that medical care would eventually be provided for all Iranians, but it will obviously be a long time before this becomes a reality. Finance has been made available to ensure that the poorest income groups can receive free medical service and treatment. For the majority of the population, however, the plans for medical insurance and pensions seem remote and insubstantial and the best security against a poverty-stricken old age is a large family. Perhaps it will require action on pensions and insurance, as well as a birth control progamme, to restrict population growth to a realistic level?

6

How They Work

ALMOST half of the Iranian workforce are employed in agriculture but agriculture contributes only 16·4 per cent to the gross national product. So rapid has been the increase in population and so dramatic the change in lifestyles, that Iran, not long ago a country entirely self-sufficient in foodstuffs and frequently with an excess for export, can no longer feed itself; during the 1970s Iran entered world commodity markets as a major purchaser of grain, meat and dairy products. About a quarter of the population are employed in manufacturing and the same percentage in service industries. It has been the policy of the Shah, and was that of his father before him, to industrialise the country as rapidly as possible. Initially, the wish was to make Iran self-sufficient; now it is to create an industrial power capable of exporting manufactured goods throughout adjacent markets.

While the fourfold increase in the price of crude oil in 1973 brought wealth to Iran to an extent previously undreamt of, the country was well on its way to becoming the Japan of the Middle East before this. The reason that Iran has been able to utilise the increased oil revenues in a way that other oil rich kingdoms have not, has been the degree to which modernisation had already gone during the post-Mossadegh era. However serious has become the shortage of skilled manpower—and it is indeed very serious—the basic infrastructure of an industrialised nation had been well established by the country's earlier Development Plan. Whereas other oil states were accumulating vast liquid assets and thereby terrifying Western economists lest they should 'play the market' for political ends, Iran has developed her programme of capital expansion almost fast enough to absorb the increased income. That which could not be absorbed was used by the Shah to buy into industry outside Iran and to provide economic support for those countries with which Iran desired closer relations.

The Shah is well aware of the ephemeral nature of his country's wealth. At present rates of extraction and with the known reserves, Iran can expect to have produced its last oil by the late 1990s. While no serious economist would wish to make exact calculations on such vague figures the general picture is widely accepted, not least by the Shah. Other Middle Eastern oil states can expect their reserves to last them longer. Away from the oil states the search for alternative energy sources is on and again, no scientist, let alone an economist, will make prognostications as to when these will be available. Iran's policy is based on alternative energy sources being found quite soon and so she is prepared to extract as much oil as possible, as quickly as possible, and for as much as it can be sold. The money so gained is being used to develop an industrial economy that will be strong enough to survive the eventual decline in oil revenues so giving Iranians the expectation of high living standards well into the twenty-first century. The Shah hopes, one suspects, that the alternative energy sources are found after he has established his industrial base but well in advance of the exhaustion of his oil supplies. In the long term, Iran's interests and those of the oil-consuming countries must be the same. Oil, so the Shah has frequently commented, is too noble a substance to be used as a fuel but should be used only for petrochemical purposes.

Given his aims, it is little wonder that the Shah is impatient. The increased oil revenues are no longer giving him, because of inflation, the purchasing power that his development plans call for. Other OPEC countries are reluctant to increase oil prices to the level which would satisfy the Shah because of their fears of inflation. With more of their assets in cash, because their economies are not able to absorb the revenues in the way in which Iran can, these countries have more to fear from inflation and the subsequent reduction in the value of their reserves. With a slowing down in capital investment programmes the time at which Iran can direct its oil away from fuel and into petro-chemical production is delayed. That this might never be possible must be the nightmare of Iranian economists.

OIL

It was in 1908 that D'Arcy first struck oil in commercial quantities at Masjid-i-Sulaiman in the southern Zagros. The Anglo-Persian Oil Company, the predecessor of BP, was formed the following year and, in 1914, the British Government purchased a £2 million controlling share in the Company to ensure adequate supplies of fuel oil for the Royal Navy. Early developments of the Persian oil-field was hindered by the difficult terrain and the need to import virtually everything that was needed from outside the country. Difficulties were further increased by the political uncertainties and in the early years the Company dealt more with the Bakhtiari chieftains than it did with the government in Tehran.

During the 1920s the oil revenues paid to the Government had fluctuated between £400,000 in 1923 and £1,437,000 in 1929. A new agreement made in 1933 gave the Government a higher and less variable income as well as other important long term considerations. In 1939 the total value of oil exports was £13·5 million, while fruit and berries at £1·3 million and carpets at £0·8 million held second and third place as national exports. Almost all of the oil exports went to the British Empire. During the war years imports by the Anglo-Persian Oil Company averaged a third of the country's total and exports two thirds, showing well how dependent Iran then was on the Company in her balance of trade.

The protection of the oil-fields was an immediate interest of the British when World War II started and became a prime reason for the Anglo-Russian occupation of 1941. Oil production having suffered a setback because of shipping difficulties in the early war years, was increased to supply the Russian Second Front and, by 1945, reached nearly 17 million tons.

In the immediate post-war period the demand for oil steadily increased and with this the revenue paid to the Iranian Government. In an attempt to force the Company to increase its payments which, in the early 1950s amounted to only 11s 6·2d (57½p) per ton, Prime Minister Mossadegh nationalised the Company. Iranian oil was immediately 'blacked' on the international market and the industry stagnated for three years with production reduced to 3 per cent of its original figure. In 1954, with Mossadegh overthrown, the Shah's government signed a new agreement with a group of British, Dutch, American and French companies, since known as The Consortium. The National Iranian Oil Company, established earlier by Mossadegh, took over all the non-basic services, much of the refinery capacity, the distribution of all oil within Iran and had its claim to own all the oil produced, acknowledged. A complicated structure of holding and marketing companies was established. 'Posted prices', that is prices published by each trading company of which 12½ per cent was paid to NIOC, together with a tax of 50 per cent of its net income, became the

---

Carpet merchants in a Tehran bazaar. The buying and selling of carpets is a national pastime in Iran and nowhere is this more so than in the numerous courtyards of the Tehran bazaar—the largest in the country. Elsewhere in the bazaar, all is hustle and noise, but amongst the carpet sellers there is an air of tranquillity and seriousness

Carpet making has been associated with Persia for centuries. In the main the craft has been practised in the home where the women have produced carpets incorporating tribal designs. During the reign of Shah Abbas, larger carpets were made, always by hand, in royal workshops, or factories. Recently the Government has established training schools to ensure that the craft continues to be taught

پازیریک
کپی فرش بافت ایران و متون نقاشی نگارگری پازیریک
کشف شده است
Copy of rug woven in Iran relating
to Achaemenian age discovered in
Pazyryk bowl

basis for new payments. The agreement was to run for twenty-five years with three further options of five years from 1979. Provision was made for the ever-increasing participation of Iranians at all levels within the industry and, by 1965, little more than 10 years after the agreement was made, less than 400 of the 30,000 employees of the Consortium were non-Iranian.

Production increased rapidly. By 1965 the daily production was approximately $\frac{3}{4}$ million barrels, giving a revenue of 40 per cent of the total national budget. In 1972–3 this had increased to 2 million barrels a day and the share of the national budget had risen to 50 per cent. At this stage the Shah began new negotiations with the Consortium. He gave them the option of either holding to the 1954 agreement until its expiration in 1979, at which time the individual members of the Consortium would have had to bid alongside all other companies for future trade, or a new agreement to come into effect immediately.

In May 1973 the Consortium entered into a fresh agreement. By this the Consortium surrendered all its rights to any resources, deposits, assets or concessions that remained under the old agreement, in exchange for a twenty-year sales contract tied to certain specific undertakings concerning investment

---

Grain is still threshed as it has been since time immemorial. The grain is stacked in circular piles some 15m in diameter and 2m in height. Oxen or horses are then driven round and through this, dragging heavy spiked rollers to separate the heads of wheat or barley from the straw. After several days of this, winnowing begins, using large wooden forks and relying on the wind to carry the chaff away as the farmers, again for days on end, toss the grain and straw into the air

Education in the use of agricultural equipment is as essential as the equipment itself. Here horses are being used to thresh grain by being driven round the threshing area in a circle, while, in the background, tractors perform exactly the same manoeuvre

levels in new projects. No sooner, it seemed, had this been completed than the Gulf States members of OPEC, in October of the same year, announced their own 'posted price' of $3·65 a barrel—an increase of 70 per cent on the earlier price.

While the Consortium, national governments and private motorists were taking stock of this and bemoaning the increase in the price of petrol from 36p to 42p per gallon the Arab-Israeli war flared up again. The Arabs placed an embargo on all oil going to countries supporting Israel. The Iranians, however, while offering the Egyptians 500,000 tons of oil, did not limit oil sales, so making it possible for the Consortium to juggle their shipping schedules to keep the consumer countries supplied. Any thanks, however, that consuming countries might have lavished on Iran were quickly withdrawn when, within weeks, the Iranians led the 'hawkish' element within the OPEC Conference at Vienna which resulted in the Christmas bombshell of 23 December 1973—a new 'posted price' of $11 for Gulf oil, representing a fourfold increase on prices prevailing only three months previously. The industrial nations shuddered, inflation galloped, the underdeveloped nations, particularly India, received setbacks which must have brought them close to despair. The Iranians, by now the world's fourth largest oil-producing, and second largest oil-exporting state, celebrated by reviewing their current five year plan to take into account an annual revenue which had increased overnight from $3·6 billion to $14 billion always providing, of course, that the sales would continue at their original level. The world could never, quite literally, be quite the same again.

The new price fixed by OPEC claimed to be based on the expected costs of alternative energy sources, a calculation vague in the extreme. What was not known was whether or not the industrial West could pay. Inflation was already rampant when the Vienna decision was announced and the new price brought many people close to panic. Assurances by the Shah that this would only lead to inflation of between 1·5 and 2 per cent did nothing to reassure economists. The industrial countries cut their demand as widespread economies were made but these were not sufficient to prevent heavy price increases in manufactured goods, many of which were just those goods which the Shah wished to buy. In the short term it seemed certain that OPEC had overreached itself.

Nearly a year after the Vienna price rise, *The Times* reported 'Iran is the most fiercely competitive and potentially one of the most rewarding countries for foreign investment in the world today. The race is on to turn what less than a generation ago was a bankrupt, essentially feudal society into an industrial power capable of holding its own with West Germany and Japan.' It continued: 'Nowhere else do the statistics so quickly become out-of-date as the economy booms at an internationally unprecedented rate'. Less than a year later *The Times* was saying, 'Today there is more caution . . . although there is not the frantic pace of the past year, there is no reason to suppose that the boom is over . . . the greatest number of "treasure hunters" or the frankly curious have largely disappeared. The city (Tehran) is left with the more serious and persistent businessman . . .'. During that year Tehran had, indeed, seen a flood of treasure-seekers. During the last ten days of May Tehran received the Moroccan Prime Minister, the Egyptian Deputy Prime Minister, the Chairman of the US Atomic Energy Commission, the Ministers of Economy from Syria, Poland, Czechoslovakia and Mexico together with trade missions from France and Turkey. At the same time Hoveyda was in Hungary negotiating a trade agreement and preparing to go to Yugoslavia the next week. The pace was far too hot. Vastly ambitious schemes were discussed but quickly ran into difficulties and most were abandoned. Many potential businessmen did not do their homework properly. 'One man even wanted to show us how to make bricks', an Iranian said, 'We've been making them for 2,500 years, somewhat longer than in his own country.' Many Iranians, too, it seemed, also thought that the new-found oil riches could easily make their way to their own pockets and hairbrain schemes so devised quickly came to nought.

Throughout 1974 off-loadings of Iranian oil, as with other

OPEC countries, fluctuated but invariably the direction was downwards. A nine-month price freeze was announced in January 1975 but consumer nations feared the round of price talks scheduled for Vienna in September. The Shah was known to be pressing for a 30 per cent increase—'to combat imported inflation'—while it was also noted that Iranian production had fallen by 11·3 per cent during the first six months of 1975. The Saudi's production had, in contrast, risen in May mainly because of the slightly lower, allowable, prices charged. Within OPEC the moderates prevailed and the price increase, widely speculated about, was limited to 10 per cent.

Towards the end of the Iranian year 1353 (1974–5) it became apparent that Iran was likely to show a deficit on its national budget. As it turned out this was not as large, $2·7 billion, as the $4 billion that had been estimated but nevertheless showed that the balmy days of 1974 were over. During the first nine months of that year foreign credits amounting to $1·2 billion had been extended to the UK, $1 billion to the IMF, $1 billion to France, $3 billion to Italy and smaller sums totalling $1·5 billion to Pakistan, India, Egypt and Syria. In addition, the Shah had purchased 25 per cent of West Germany's vast Krupp industrial empire. These, the *Middle East Economic Digest* noted, 'are turning points in relations between the industrial West and what used to be known as the underdeveloped world. It marks the final, if reluctant, acceptance by major industrial states of a new and equal relationship which recognises the interdependence of consumers and producers of basic raw materials.'

During 1976 Iran's need for ready cash again became evident. In February there had been talk that she would not be able to complete the loan promised to the UK and a threat that she would not be able to honour all contracts for industrial goods that had recently been signed. This appeared to be part of the pressure that Iran was putting on the Consortium and national Governments to increase their purchasing of Iranian oil which had suffered an 11 per cent fall during the previous year. The budget for 1976–7 would have to be cut in the light of this,

Majidi had said in January. The purchase of six Spruance-class Destroyers from the US was threatened. The plan for increasing the capacity of the telephone service by 1978 was delayed until 1980. 'If you want to sell us more', said Hoveyda in February, 'you'd better buy more oil'. In March the Shah refused to meet the leaders of the Consortium when they visited Tehran. In April, $200 million of credits from France were recalled, in May negotiations for a $750 million Eurodollar loan were thought to be taking place as well as negotiations for a loan of $1·2 billion from Saudi Arabia. Two months later NIOC were looking for a $2·1 billion loan for pipeline construction. The Consortium said that it could not afford to contribute the 40 per cent required by the 1973 agreement for new capital needed in the oil industry to enable further production units to be brought on stream.

While there were obvious strains showing in the economy these should not be exaggerated. The general budget presented to the *Majlis* for 1976–7 was for $27·6 billion with an expected deficit, admittedly the first one to be planned for in six years, of $2·4 billion. It is likely that some of the more grandiose schemes inaugurated earlier will be shelved or even cancelled. The future purchasing of Concorde, the building of the new Tehran airport, perhaps even the turbo train to link Mashad to Tehran could come under the axe. In November 1975 the Shah established a Royal Commission to oversee and vet development projects—its personnel have the teeth to make sure that its recommendations are followed. Iran is a very rich country and growing richer but the dependence on oil, now at 86 per cent of Government revenue—its highest ever— means that this new note of caution is most welcome.

THE FIFTH FIVE-YEAR PLAN—MARCH 1973 TO MARCH 1978

The Fifth Five-Year Plan was approved in late 1972; it is of especial interest as it was produced before the increased revenues were available. A huge increase in investment from

$11 billion in the previous plan to $32 billion was the central feature of the proposals. Oil receipts were expected to amount to $22 billion during the five-year period, so accounting for 78 per cent of revenue; 14 per cent of revenue was expected to come from non-oil exports while the remaining 8 per cent would come from 'invisibles'—tourism, in particular, was expected to boom. It was calculated that the GNP would double during the period so giving a growth rate of 11·4 per cent, an increase in per capita income from $513 to $907 and the creation of new jobs at the rate of 1,000 a day. A more equitable distribution of the nation's wealth between both rich and poor and between urban and rural dwellers was to be effected. Industry was to receive the highest level of investment at $6·7 billion, closely followed by housing with $5·4 billion. Investment in the oil industry was fixed at $4·4 billion with the intention of increasing output to 8·3 million barrels a day and doubling refinery capacity by 1978. Agriculture received $2·35 billion in order that it could achieve a growth rate of 5 per cent, in contrast to 3 per cent in the previous five years. Education was in fifth place with $1·7 billion. Premier Hoveyda called for 'discipline as a moral responsibility' and urged 'frugality, revolutionary self-abnegation, a shunning of luxuries and a dedication to the cause of making Iran great, prosperous and prestigious once again'.

Following the Agreement with the Consortium in May 1973 the Shah said of the Plan: 'Although it is only a few short months since this Plan was discussed at Persepolis and we approved it, I can tell you now that that Plan has in fact become outdated'. Noting that the new Agreement 'would put considerably higher revenues at Iran's disposal', the Shah charged PBO to revise the Plan. There then followed the price rises of October and December.

PBO considered various proposals which would have called for fixed public capital investment at three levels: $29·8 billion, $45 billion and $55 billion. While the money might, under the ambitious thinking of the time, have been available for the highest of these figures, it was realised that there were basic constraints on the economy which a surfeit of money could not overcome. Chief of these was the shortage of skilled manpower, followed by infrastructure weaknesses particularly in communications. A prime concern was the inevitable inflationary nature of such an investment programme.

The Revised Plan was presented to the Shah in August 1974. It was based on fixed capital investment by the government of $45 billion, with a further $23 billion of investment channelled through the private sector. The new proposals provided for a mammoth annual growth of 25·9 per cent in real terms with the expectation that per capita incomes will reach $1,521 by 1978. Priority in development was to be given to those industries in which Iran has a natural cost advantage by using local raw materials. These were seen as being oil, gas, iron, steel and copper. Virtually no limit was to be placed on investment in industries processing these materials providing that other aspects of the industrial infrastructure could tolerate this. Particular attention, therefore, was to be directed at all levels of communications, most specifically the southern ports and their links with the rest of the country.

A second priority was given to development schemes already started where agreements existed for these with other countries. This was followed by a special commitment to the farming community to raise living standards and per capita output to considerably higher levels than had been originally postulated. A further commitment was made to raise the living standards, particularly of the lowest income levels, by increasing job and educational opportunities, expanding health and welfare services and providing adequate and cheap food, housing, transport and other basic needs. In presenting the Plan, Majidi drew attention to the inflationary nature of the programme and cautioned that this might increase the economic gap between different social groups, a possibility which he hoped to prevent by expanded welfare and social services.

The Shah told the Ramsar Conference summoned to receive this new Plan:

> *Patriotism should have a proper place but today I would condense this by saying that the opportunities in such areas do not occur in all countries at all times. It is only rarely that the era and the possibility coincides as they have fortunately done in our case and it would be a pity not to use these opportunities properly. Today we do not expect Iranians to tighten their belts and eat less to reach a Utopia which is elusive year after year. We do not promise them prosperity in the future but are trying to give them prosperity today as far as is within our means.*

The Shah continued:

> *It is our hope that we should adopt the advanced technological civilisation of the outside world and make the most of it. But at the same time we should try to see that the drawbacks or even corruptions that usually accompany advanced technological civilisation do not find their way into our country.*

The Plan dominates all aspects of economic affairs. With such a growth rate it is difficult to take stock of what is actually happening at the present, particularly in the industrial sphere where changes are the most rapid. That not all, if any, of the aims of the Plan are achieved by 1978 hardly matters. The planning for the Sixth Plan will surely be a further revision and refinement of the present intention. Whatever are the reservations about statistics in the Iranian situation, and Curzon once noted that 'these are in their essences an insult to the Oriental imagination', it is undoubtedly the Revised Plan that now controls the day-to-day affairs of the Iranian people.

AGRICULTURE

The White Revolution has certainly changed life in rural Iran. The large estates have virtually disappeared and the era of the peasant owning the land he works has begun. While ownership patterns have indeed changed, agricultural production has lagged behind all other aspects of the country's economy. The rural/urban imbalance has continued virtually unchanged, giving salaries in the ratio of 1:5 or 6, while the bottom 30 per cent of the wage-earning sector, almost entirely country folk, account for only 8 per cent of consumption.

Centuries of suppression have made it difficult for the peasant farmers to take the initiative in this new situation. Having purchased their farms with huge government loans, they have had to be coaxed and cajoled into more modern techniques. The Literacy Corps and the Agricultural Advisers have indeed helped but there has remained the need for large and well directed credits and for a new decision-making infrastructure to develop in the villages to replace the *malek* (landlord). In the better regulated villages the *malek* had provided the capital, organised market outlets and provided some form of social entity to the community; in areas where the *malek* had been weak, cruel or disinterested, the community had suffered immensely. But centuries of such a regime have given the peasant farmers no legacy of organisational ability on which to build once he owned his own land. The village headmen—the *kadkhodas*—and the chairmen of the village councils—*raisi anjeman*—have had difficulty establishing their authority.

Rural co-operatives were founded with government loans to assist with marketing while loans were also made for the acquisition of capital equipment. The farmers have been slow to respond, while government officials have not always appreciated the problems which the villages face. The task of educating such a vast number of farmers has until now really defeated the system. The output per capita has remained very low but then Iran has been faced with the problem with which all countries whose economy develops fast have had to come to terms—if agricultural production becomes efficient where do the redundant farmers go?

Not until the Plan did it look as if agriculture was to be given the opportunity of dropping its Cinderella image. Despite the reforms and innovations of the 1960s, production had only increased at three per cent per annum. Not only does Iran need to feed itself, its economic advisers maintain, it also needs to raise the living standards of its rural community so that they can afford to absorb the products of the industrial growth in the cities.

Iran is now coming to terms with the economic results of the social and political aims of the White Revolution and their consequence amongst the farming community. The size of landholding is, on average, too small and too scattered to make it possible to mechanise the unit effectively. There are too many villages and far too many of them are too small. Current policy is shifting away from small co-operatives in favour of fewer, larger, marketing organisations. In some cases co-operatives are being succeeded by farm corporations, even by agro-industrial units.

The rural Iranian does not understand this. His expectations were raised by owning his own land. He accepted the propaganda that he heard on his transistor radio and was led to expect a veritable rural utopia. The installation of a piped water supply, the lectures on fertilisers, better animal husbandry and human hygiene encouraged him to believe that this ideal was coming close to reality. Now some are getting suspicious. Why is it, they say, that some of the villages are being encouraged to grow larger and now have a school, a clinic, a government vet, even a doctor, and perhaps some new-styled houses, whereas they have had nothing since the arrival of the water scheme? Endless meetings of village headmen and government advisers leave them, as they do most country folk, with a sense of frustration and annoyance.

By aiming at such an increase in food production, the Plan, without saying so in as many words, is making a fundamental change in rural Iran. Not even if all the oil revenues were deployed to raising the standard of living in the country could all 50,000 villages have all the facilities they believe they need, nor would it make economic sense. Instead, certain villages, on the basis of local as well as general statistical criteria, are being selected as growth centres. In these villages centralised facilities are being provided such as schools, clinics and light industry and investment generally is being made freely available. Those villages conveniently situated to the growth centres and with populations in excess of 250 are being developed as 'satellites', having a smaller number of facilities. Those villages with fewer people are receiving only limited assistance, probably only a water supply system and their inhabitants—with good reason—feel that their village is being left to die and their people are being encouraged to move away. So far there are just over a thousand such schemes, involving about 12,000 villages.

An improvement in agricultural production necessitates an improved distribution network if a greater share of the final price is to be returned to the producer. The membership of rural co-operatives is expected to grow from 1·8 million to 3 million but the number of co-operative units is to be reduced from 8,000 to 3,000. It is intended that these will be further consolidated into 150 Co-operative Federations. During the early 1970s a number of farm corporations were established. This, more specialised and larger-scaled farming than any known in Iran in the past, could well be the pattern for the future. A further 100 units—there are currently forty-three— are planned before 1978 with a combined area of 420,000 hectares. In addition, a further 300,000 hectares of agro-industrial and meat and dairy complexes are planned. Both farm corporations and agro-industrial complexes are a clear reflection of the need to increase agricultural output and are a response that is strictly economic, if also revolutionary.

If the sceptic scoffs at the scale of the proposed change, so be it, as he will undoubtedly be right in many instances; but change there will be as the economy now looks to massive investment in this, the most established and reactionary area of the economy. The specific aims are to raise cereal production from 5·6 million tons to 8·6 million, industrial crops from 5·1 million tons to 8·5 million, orchard fruit from 1·8 million tons to 2·4 million, vegetables and soft fruit from 3·2 million tons to 3·6 million, red meat from 305,000 tons to 519,000, milk from 1·9 million tons to 2·8 million and poultry from 50,000 tons to 200,000 tons

In the meantime, Iran continues to import large quantities of foodstuffs and is planning silos capable of holding a minimum of four months' supply of essential commodities. As Iran's hunger increases so it is in everyone's interests that her agriculture also improves. Subsistence, or near subsistence, farming is rapidly giving way to the wage-earning agricultural labourer—or will it be operative?

Perhaps not everyone is convinced by such grandiose schemes and the Empress, while visiting the villages in the Kavir in the summer of 1976, hinted at this. She suggested that the newly proposed Institute for Rural Research should consider whether it is 'better to go for the most modern technology and machinery, or is it possible to discover a small-scale technology more suited to Iranian conditions and to the scale of Iranian agriculture? Are there', she continued, 'forms of local government that will permit a greater amount of decision-making authority to be handed to the villages themselves?'

THE POWER BASE

In water-starved Europe of 1976 it was perhaps easier than it had been to understand that, since time immemorial, water has meant wealth in Iran. Precipitation over the country averages 240mm, but more than half of this falls on the Caspian lowlands, an area comprising less than 1 per cent of the whole. The building of *qanats* was the traditional and unique Iranian response to this climatic problem. It is estimated that there are some 50,000 of these, though only about a tenth are of real significance; they have an average length of 5km but the longest is more that 70km. They deliver about 2 per cent of the available water supply and made possible the irrigation of 2 million hectares of land by the start of the Pahlavi era.

The building of dams and the regulation of water has since increased the area of irrigated land to 3·5 million hectares, a figure due to rise to 4 million hectares by 1978. This will also provide sufficient water for an urban population of 17 million, satisfy the needs of the rapidly expanding industrial sector as well as increasing HEP (hydro-electric power) potential by 125 per cent. Longer term plans look to a utilisation of 85 per cent of available surface water which, optimists say, could supply 18 million hectares of land. In the meantime, Tehran still wonders if the immediate proposals can slake its ever-increasing thirst.

Capital investment in water storage is colossal. During the past fifty years water storage has increased fourteenfold through the building of such dams as the Shahbanou Farah Dam on the Sephid Rud, the Mohammed Reza Shah Pahlavi Dam at Dezful and the Amir Kabir Dam at Karaj. More dams are being built: the vast Reza Shah the Great Dam in Khuzestan, the Lar Dam, the Gheshlaq, the Pisheen and the Minab Dams should almost double the existing capacity by 1983. Of these schemes, that in Khuzestan is the largest, where the Karum river will be impounded giving a storage capacity of 2·9 billion cubic metres and where the HEP capacity at 6 billion kilowatts could repay the total construction costs, at constant prices, in eighteen months.

A fourfold increase in the domestic use of oil and oil products took place in the ten years prior to 1975. Expectations are that this market will continue to grow at 17·8 per cent annually. In order to achieve this the refinery capacity is to be increased from 250,000 barrels a day to 655,000 barrels by 1978; this will involve both increasing the capacity of existing refineries and building new ones in Tabriz and Isfahan. Considerable investment is being made in expanding the oil pipeline network. Tank farm capacity is to be increased to 4 million cubic metres. Geological searches are being undertaken for new oil fields. Great emphasis, as has already been noted, is being placed on the growth of the petrochemical industry. NIOC are now joint partners in a number of exploration schemes outside Iran, chiefly with BP in the North Sea, and are building a London office on the corner of Victoria Street and Tothill Street—facing the House of Commons! Iran's tanker fleet, which came into operation only in 1976 by the purchase of five tankers from BP, will be increased to a capacity of about 1 million tons.

Iran's reserves of natural gas are vast: some estimates suggest that there is sufficient to supply the energy requirements of the country for 300 years and, however arbitrary this figure may be, it is reasonably certain that the reserves are second only to those of Russia. Gas is found in association with oil and by itself; where in association with oil it must be extracted at the same time. Until the use of gas for domestic purposes in Shiraz in 1963, but more especially until the completion of the gas pipe-line to the USSR in 1970, the gas was 'burnt off' at the well head as the oil was removed. This was probably the greatest ever wastage of energy resources in the world's history. The capital cost of utilising this was colossal but the revenue so earned quickly ensured a dividend on the pipeline installation cost. In December 1974 the Iranians eventually forced a new agreement on the USSR for a price of 57 cents a 1,000 cubic metres of gas, against the original 30 cents, and agreed to an annual sale of 13 billion cubic metres. Much of this gas finds its way to eastern Europe. In addition to supplying gas to the USSR, the pipeline supplies Iranian industries on the main north/south axial route, particularly the Isfahan steel complex.

Great importance is being attached to the use of gas in the petrochemical industry, as well as in the production of electricity, where it is expected to provide approximately a quarter of the nation's requirements by 1978. The growth in the use of electricity has been prodigious, while projections for growth between 1973 and 1978 are at a massive 31 per cent per annum. Generating capacity during the same period is to increase at 36 per cent. In March 1976 the Minister for Energy, Iraj Vahidi, spoke of a twenty-year energy master plan which would aim at integrating alternative energy sources at the earliest opportunity and conserving fossil fuels for petrochemical use. Short-term increases in the use of natural gas are envisaged to economise on oil but eventually this, too, will be replaced. The limited reserves of coal will be conserved for use in the steel industry. Nuclear energy is to be developed so that, according to Vahidi, it will be the leading source of energy in two decades. Expansion of HEP and research into use of solar energy are expected.

Currently work is taking place on the construction of eighteen gas-powered generators each with a capacity of 25 megawatts and nine larger generators each with a capacity of 45 megawatts. Large scale diesel-powered generator schemes are now being installed in Mashad, Ahvaz, Isfahan and Mazanderan. Numerous smaller generating projects are under way in towns and villages throughout the land. Thermal generating capacity is being quadrupled during the period of the Plan. HEPs contribution to generating capacity will more than double during the same period mainly due to the generators at the Reza Shah the Great Dam. Almost as much money as that invested in generating capacity is being spent on transmission and distribution networks.

The Shah has frequently spoken about the need to develop alternative energy sources, singling out nuclear power for special attention. A small reactor has been used for research purposes at Tehran University since the early 1960s, but significant investment in the nuclear age is very recent. Currently, Iran has three major contracts in the nuclear energy field. AEO (Atomic Energy Organisation) signed an outline agreement with France in 1974 for five nuclear power stations at a cost of $1·2 billion; two of these (900 megawatt capacity) are planned for the Karum river and Bushehr. The second agreement was with West Germany for two more plants to be operational by 1980 and 1981 and a third agreement with the UK for a joint research programme and training facilities for Iranians at Harwell. Negotiations are taking place with the US for a massive deal involving eight reactors.

Meanwhile, the immediate situation is one of shortfall in power supplies as the demand from industry exceeds that which can be produced by existing generating capacity. Power cuts became a feature of Tehran in the summer of 1976 as demand exceeded supply by 300,000kw a day. Newspapers called for industrial energy consumption to be cut during the evening peak period, with the suggestion that such industries as work round the clock should install their own generators, while others should plan their schedules better to take advantage of off-peak periods. The domestic consumer, however, was not asked to economise.

INDUSTRY

The Iranian industrial scene presents many striking contrasts. For centuries industry was intrinsically linked to the bazaars, where the specialist crafts of coppersmiths, carpenters, weavers and potters were regulated by strict guild regulations. Trade with Europe resulted in small factories being established as early as the seventeenth century but, in reality, these were little more than the collecting into one place of many people who practised their traditional crafts without regard to large scale production. Factories, as currently defined, were first introduced by Reza Shah but, lacking finance, these were few in number. During the late 1950s and throughout the 1960s, major industrial units were established, mainly by foreign companies. The development of these has followed a recognisable pattern: initially they have been assembly plants for parts manufactured entirely outside Iran but, as time has passed more and more of the parts have been manufactured in the country under licence until, eventually, the entire product is Iranian. Those small industrial processes associated with the bazaars are practised

———

His Imperial Majesty Mohammed Reza Shah Pahlavi, Shahanshah of Iran

Chahar Bagh School, Isfahan. One of the many elaborate inlaid vaulted ceilings which, since the time of Shah Abbas, have made the buildings of Isfahan a delight to resident and visitor alike

throughout the country; the larger units introduced before 1960 were sited almost exclusively in the Tehran area. Since then policy has been to encourage the growth of other industrial centres, mainly around major cities and oil-fields, but Tehran has continued to dominate. A country as large as Iran, with communications as limited as they have been, precludes the growth of many industrial centres and, despite the legislation, it would seem as if the dominance of the capital will continue. It will be many years before the manufacture in Tehran of, say, kitchen implements, will replace the bazaar craftsman making his pots in far-off Sistan.

The rapid development of the industrial sector continues to be the prime consideration of government policy. Existing industry is to be modernised so as to make economies in production and improve quality. New industry will be developed both in relation to that which already exists and with an eye to export opportunities. Emphasis is being placed on the amalgamation of small units, the vertical integration of processes and the establishment of large fully integrated industrial complexes. Tariffs are to be regulated so as to raise the standard of home-produced goods by making them competitive with those imported. A review is being made of commercial banking

---

The refinery at Abadan was developed by the old Anglo-Persian Oil Company and came on stream in 1911. For many years it was the world's largest refinery. During World War II, oil products from Abadan were of the utmost importance to the Allies

The oil fields occupy only a small area of Iran and employ relatively few people. Their value to the economy, of course, is immense. Because the oil fields are situated in the comparatively inaccessible and underdeveloped south-west, the gas was, for a long time, simply burnt off at the well heads. Now, this very valuable commodity is piped to markets in both Iran and the USSR and is as important to the economy as oil

H

operations to ensure a more careful appraisal of potential investment projects. Particular attention is to be given to improving the standard of management and basic skills. 'In the past, managers had a limited outlook on efficiency, but managers of today should expand their views to embrace all social factors, including the interests of society, in determining their approach to efficiency', noted the Shah.

Great emphasis has been placed by Iranian economists on the creation of a major iron and steel industry. The Aryamehr steel plant at Isfahan, Iran's first, came into operation in 1973. Initially, it was designed to produce 600,000 tons per annum but this figure has constantly been revised as further investment in the plant has been made. In 1973–4 the plant produced a quarter of a million tons of steel. Iron ore is found in sizeable reserves near Kerman as well as at Yazd, but these supplies were supplemented in 1975 when an agreement was made with India whereby Iran could purchase up to 7·5 million tons of iron ore per annum from the Indian mines at Kudremukh. A second steel plant at Ahvaz started production in 1974. Further plants are either being built, or being planned, at Bandar Abbas, Kangan, Isfahan and in Khorasan. The new mill in Isfahan is scheduled for completion in 1980 with a planned annual production of 1·2 million tons; that at Bandar Abbas, sited with the export market in mind, has an annual production target of 3 million tons. Total production from all units is set at 10 million tons by 1978, by which time it is expected to satisfy the domestic demand for constructional steel, pipes, wire and cable. Projections in the industry are notoriously difficult to make; those made by the chairman of NISIC (National Iranian Iron and Steel Industries Company) in December 1974 sited a production of between 14–17 million tons by 1983 giving it 'the most ambitious steel development plan in the Middle East'. The Arak Aluminium plant has a capacity of 45,000 tons and considerable quantities of aluminium ingots are exported. The Sar Cheshmeh copper deposits near Kerman are expected to yield 145,000 tons per annum of blister copper through the ore concentration plant to be built there by 1978.

The automobile industry started in a small way with the assembly of foreign-made parts, under licence, in Tehran in 1960. Iran National, which now co-ordinates the industry, produced almost 100,000 units in 1975–6 under a system which is giving an ever-increasing Iranian element to the manufacturing process. 'Assembly', said the Chairman, 'will soon be forgotten from the vocabulary'. The Plan aims at seventy-five per cent of Iranian-produced parts by 1978. Development plans are vastly ambitious. Iran National talks of production rising to half a million by 1980 with Iran becoming a major car exporter. During 1974 the Toyota Company of Japan was asked to design a plant capable of producing 250,000 units per annum within five years, a scheme which the Japanese claimed was 'quite impossible'. Currently, Mercedes-Benz, British Leyland, Chrysler, Fiat and other cars are manufactured in Iran. The most popular car is the Peykan, based on the Hillman Hunter. With increasing affluence, a completely new class of car owner becomes a possibility: '. . . every building worker in Tehran', a jaundiced reporter wrote recently, 'will pull out a packet of cigarettes and consider whether or not to buy a Peykan'.

Lorries, buses and vanettes are also made under licence. Despite a massive increase in production, large numbers of lorries and buses have been ordered from the US and UK. The Tabriz Tractor Plant, with an original capacity of 5,000 a year, is expected to produce 20,000 a year by 1978. Austrian State Railways are now building a rolling-stock factory at Arak, capable of producing 1,000 waggons a year. A dry dock, capable of taking supertankers of up to 500,000 tons, is being built at Bandar Abbas; this will provide a much-needed service in the Gulf and that part of the Indian Ocean. Shipbuilding facilities for boats of up to 6,000 tons are also to be provided.

It is in the building industry that the greatest changes and confusion are to be seen; it is not just in the contrasts in building techniques which see elaborate steel structures being lifted into place using rope and wooden scaffold poles of precarious type, but in the apparent contradiction in planning controls. The industry cannot expand fast enough to satisfy the enormous demands; planning is all too often overtaken by events. Supplies of building materials are always in short supply—particularly cement. The shortage of skilled and semi-skilled workers is even graver than that of materials. The shortfall in office and residential accommodation will last for a long time, as the demand for government building projects would appear to have tied up the industry far into the future. A sizeable tax advantage was announced recently to encourage private enterprise to build high-rise office blocks. Two commercial banks, the Construction Bank and the Construction Investment Bank, were formed in 1976 to encourage private investment in the industry. Taxes on imported prefabricated houses have been virtually abolished in an attempt to alleviate the shortage in residential accommodation.

The postal service dates back to some very shaky beginnings in the late nineteenth century and Persia joined the International Postal Union in 1877. The service is still in need of much improvement. The Plan calls for massive reorganisation 'to create the necessary dynamism', the setting up of a special company to deal with the distribution of mail and for mechanical mail sorting in the major cities. It calls for 'the establishment of 300 urban post offices . . . 245 letter delivery stations . . . and 16,000 post office boxes'. If all this comes about, and deliveries are expected to take a maximum of forty-eight hours between towns, what will happen to that most lethargic of all Persian workers—the post office counter clerk? The telephone system was deplorable until the introduction of the inter-city microwave system in 1972. Improvements, constantly promised, seem always to be delayed. It is frequently easier to make an international call from Tehran, routed through the satellite tracking station outside Hamedan, than it is to get certain numbers within the city. Despite all the sophisticated equipment which has been installed recently it remains very difficult and expensive for a private individual to have a new telephone installed— and the delay seems to be getting longer, rather than shorter.

It is to the petrochemical industry that Iran is looking for its future prosperity. The industry really dates from the establishment of the artificial fertiliser plant at Shiraz in 1966, a plant recently expanded as a result of an agreement with Rumania. The National Petrochemical Company (NPC) works through joint holding companies; the Abadan Petrochemical Company with B. F. Goodrich; the Kharg Chemical Company with Amoco International and the Shahpur Chemical Company with Allied Chemicals. A large number of new projects are under way; two of these are in Bandar Shahpur. The larger one, with Mitsui of Japan is a $1 billion complex, producing caustic soda and liquefied petroleum gas and derivatives, while the other, smaller, project set up by the Iran-Nippon Company will produce, amongst other things, 45,000 tons of di-octyphthalate. Currently, NPC is negotiating with Cabot International of the USA, with Bayer of West Germany, with a number of Japanese firms and with Dow Chemicals. Early in 1976, the government stated that the industry would be developed according to a threefold classification: the production of basic chemicals would remain the preserve of NPC and government finance; the manufacture of medium range products would be open to joint investment schemes, possibly with foreign companies, whilst the third area would be the production of chemical products for the consumer market, where private investment would be expected. Government investment is expected to be $4.5 billion over five years. Long-term projects look very much to the export market and by 1983 Iran expects to be producing between 5 and 10 per cent of the world's petrochemical requirements. International companies have reacted rapidly to this expanding area for investment.

Alongside the growth in the manufacturing industries has been an equal growth in service and consumer-based industries. Expansion in Government agencies, national and international company offices, hotel and conference complexes have all required large numbers of services which, until very recently, were unknown in Iran. Advertising agencies, personnel management consultancies, catering companies, night clubs and the like are new to the Iranian scene. There is a grave shortage of good secretaries. A more opulent and clothes-conscious society has revitalised the textile industry and revolutionised the shoe industry. All forms of food processing industries are booming at an unprecedented rate. Distribution networks struggle to keep up with the ever-increasing requirements of public demand. More and more Iranians can afford to take holidays or pilgrimages and there is a consequent increase in those industries associated with travel and holiday accommodation.

It has been in the service industry sector that women have found an expanding labour market in recent years. The growth in women's legal rights, however, seems to have come faster than society's acceptance of women in employment. Moving from a totally male-orientated Islamic society in the 1920s to the granting of female suffrage in 1963 and legislation for equal pay in 1974 Iranian women have not taken up employment, or have not been allowed to do so by their husbands, at a level commensurate with their freedom. The female activity rate was 9·2 per cent in 1956, 13·6 per cent in 1974 and is expected to rise to 15·3 per cent by 1978. The figure for men is 77 per cent. A recent survey amongst Iranian 'top people' revealed all the prejudices against employing women that would have been found in a traditional Western society twenty years ago. MCP (Male Chauvinist Pigs) would seem to be as prevalent in Iranian society now as they have been elsewhere and the Iranian male as determined to keep his wife in the home and his girlfriend elsewhere, as any other race. It is estimated that some 500,000 women work in industry, 50,000 as secretaries, 50,000 as salesgirls, dressmakers, hairdressers, hotel personnel and the like, and some 55,000 as teachers. No more than 300 were classified as 'managers'.

The champion of women's rights is undoubtedly Princess Ashraf. 'Iranian women were granted full legal and civil rights by the Pahlavi dynasty's rulers', she said. 'But, since they received those rights without making any effort or struggle on their own part, they are sometimes apathetic and indifferent to the value of their rights and to the importance of exercising them responsibly and productively.' But the weight of centuries of being assigned to child-bearing and home-running will take a long time to break. Jobs which were held outside the home, the Princess said, 'do not detract from the solidarity of the family, but actually contributed to the welfare and happiness of every family member'.

A number of recommendations have been submitted to the *Majlis* for changes in the legal status of women. A married women's property rights bill promoted uproar in a chamber which was almost a male preserve. The traditional base of marriage must now be considered as much under attack, if not more so, in Iran as it is anywhere else. Recently, a figure of 16,000 divorces a year has been recorded giving a divorce rate of 1 in 4 of all marriages—and the figure is thought to be much higher in Tehran.

An increasing number of mixed marriages takes place each year, mainly it seems to Americans and West Germans. The attitudes of the foreign wife are a major contributory cause to the changing pattern of Iranian family life. Ettela'at said:

> *Most of the foreign wives have a job, either in their embassies or cultural relation societies . . . Even under equal conditions they command higher salaries than their Iranian counterparts . . . More important is their treatment by their husband. The average Iranian husband becomes kinder, though occasionally given to bullying; and mostly he becomes a true companion for the foreign wife, to the extent that she becomes the envy of other Iranian wives.*

The role of women will change, perhaps at a faster rate than that suggested by the Plan, as bored young Iranian housewives seek to emulate the more emancipated and economically independent Western woman.

INDUSTRIAL INVESTMENT

An edict issued in 1973, now referred to as the 13th Principle of the Shah-People Revolution, was intended to broaden the basis of industrial ownership. By this edict, since incorporated in the Plan, 99 per cent of the shares of public companies and 49 per cent of those in private companies are to be sold to the general public. The stated intention of this was to give a more equitable distribution of the benefits of industrial progress but also, of course, it is bound to make the average Iranian financially interested in maintaining the political basis of private enterprise. It is expected that some 320 private companies, many with foreign investments, will have complied with this regulation by October 1978; in many instances the companies are doubling their capital by selling new shares to the public. Share ceilings have been fixed for foreign investment which vary according to the industry: 15 per cent in food and textiles, 20 per cent in leather and metals and 25 per cent in most other sectors. The petrochemical industry is an exception at 50 per cent. Under the original proposals a maximum holding for an individual was set at R500,000 ($7,000). Workers can borrow money at 4 per cent to purchase shares.

The machinery making all this possible is the Tehran Stock Exchange, set up in 1968. The amount of business handled by the Exchange rose only slowly with some thirty-four companies having negotiable shares by 1974. However in that year two Iranian firms joined with Meryll Lynch of the US to form stock brokerage within Iran and recent years have seen a steady increase in business. In January 1974, all restrictions on the movement of capital in and out of Iran were removed and a number of major investment companies set up joint holdings with Iranian companies.

7

How They Learn

More than half the Iranian population is less than eighteen years old, 62 per cent of those over seven are illiterate; the average Iranian spends less than two seconds a year reading a book—just a few statistics illustrating the enormity of the task that faces educationalists in Iran at present. The biggest constraint on development, as has already been noted, is the shortage of skilled manpower and it is to the educational sector that Iran now looks for—inevitably—an immediate solution.

The problem is complex. There is little tradition of education within Iran; fifty years ago there were less than 10,000 secondary school places and only 40,000 primary school places in the whole country. It is out of this preciously small reservoir of educated people that the senior administrators, executives, deputies and senators have to be drawn. Population growth has outstripped the best efforts to eradicate illiteracy so that there are now more illiterates than there were ten years ago. Until recently, there has been insufficient money to build enough schools and to train the teachers, while the scattered nature of the population and reactionary attitudes to education have made the task still harder. University expansion has been rapid but, all too frequently, the qualifications gained have been irrelevant to the country's needs or, being highly marketable, have led to the graduates emigrating.

A number of schools had been established in Persia by missionaries during the nineteenth century and these offered the first real alternatives to the education provided by the priests in the *maqtabs* (village schools) and *madrasas* (theological colleges).

The most famous of the mission schools was Elburz College founded in 1898 by an American, Dr Samuel Jourdan. It was his intention to provide an education that would make it unnecessary for wealthy Persians to send their sons to Europe or Russia because 'the young oriental educated in Western lands as a rule gets out of touch with his own country . . .'. Other schools, frequently associated with hospitals, were founded by Protestant, Catholic and Nestorian missionaries. Enterprising merchants, particularly in Azarbaijan and Gilan, opened their own schools but these, together with many of the mission schools, were frequently shortlived.

The Ministry of Education was only established in 1911 and ten years later controlled 612 schools. Reza Shah was most concerned to educate the people and modelled his schools on the *écoles primaires* and the *lycées* of France; when he abdicated there were more than 250,000 children in the former and 60,000 in the Persian equivalent to the *lycée*. In 1933 he formed the Teachers' Training College in Tehran and the following year the Tehran University was established. By 1960 the number of pupils in primary schools had quadrupled to a million, while those following some form of *lycée* or high-school education numbered nearly a quarter of a million. Impressive as these figures were, they were not sufficient to create even basic literacy; furthermore, the students were found almost exclusively in the urban areas and virtually no education was available in the villages.

As part of the White Revolution legislation of 1963, the Shah created the Literacy Corps as a means of spreading basic literacy teaching to the most remote areas of the country. In many ways this resembled a military version of the British VSO and the American Peace Corps, both being developed at the same time. All High School students, on being called up for National Service, were given some basic military skills and then drafted to the villages as teachers under military discipline. Since the scheme was initiated more than 100,000 corps men, and since 1969 corps women, have been involved. Young, urban-trained and mainly enthusiastic for the ideals of the

Shah's policy, the contribution these people have made to the levels of literacy in rural areas has been immense. Wearing military uniforms, their rifles leant against the blackboards on which they were writing before classes made up of villagers of all ages, they have been one of the most inspiring of recent sights in Iran. Their contribution has, however, been far greater than just teaching literacy and numeracy skills—Schumacher must be proud of their contribution to intermediate technology. They have organised the building of their own schools and repaired others, while by 1973, so a government report states, they have built 3,000 mosques, organised the repair and construction of some 150,000km of minor roads, built 52,000 bridges and planted nearly 4 million trees! Impressive indeed, but not as significant as the political and economic ideas about which they talked with the villagers in the long hours after lessons in village houses, market places or fields. As instruments of change, the Literacy Corps has revolutionised the attitudes of the villagers to a greater extent than probably even the Shah had dreamt.

The growth in formal education during the same period has been immense: in 1963 there were 2·1 million students in full-time education, 10 years later the number was 5·2 million while the autumn term of 1976 started with 7·7 million and the number is expected to reach 12 million by 1981. The teaching profession has been unable to cope. Just over 7,000 teachers qualified in 1976, hardly sufficient to replace natural wastage in a profession of 200,000, leaving some 40,000 vacancies unfilled in the country's schools.

The entry requirements to teachers' training colleges have been low and teachers have been held in low esteem for years. There are very few graduate teachers. Many reasons have been given for this: an unexciting career structure, poor working conditions, low salaries and a labour market offering great opportunities in other areas. It will take some time for the recent infusion of vast sums of money into equipment, salaries and training to show results. In the meanwhile, it must remain doubtful if the profession can respond effectively to what is being asked of it.

The older schools are of the most rudimentary design: large classrooms, wooden desks, wide corridors, limited toilet accommodation and poor, if not non-existent, play facilities. Village schools built recently are better but still very overcrowded. City schools vary immensely, from the frankly Dickensian (whose problems are further compounded by the heat and smells of summer) to the modern prestige schools currently being built in the best residential areas. Equipment, until very recently, has been limited to blackboards and a few indifferent textbooks. The government is now investing heavily in television as a means of spreading high-quality teaching to the remotest areas. All forms of audio-visual equipment are being purchased. An appeal has gone out to all interested in writing textbooks to pool their efforts with ministry officials. 'Our textbooks', said a high school student, 'are rich in pages but poor in information'. Better libraries are being built. The tribal schools, however, remain mainly nomadic and their facilities almost non-existent. The Shah noted this and compared their results with other schools: '90 per cent of tribal high school students pass University entrance examinations', he said and went on to suggest that this might be because their teachers were not as concerned 'with appearances, luxury, welfare, comfort and outright laziness', as other teachers.

Despite all the new buildings, many children of compulsory age are not in school. Nearly 2 million, mainly those living in rural areas, of an age to be in first cycle schools in the autumn of 1976 were not in fact there, while the enrolment of 1·3 million in guidance schools and 0·7 million in high schools shows that a large number of potential students are not being educated. This is not always because of insufficient places: in some areas truancy is a significant factor as parents fail to appreciate the value of education. There is a marked shortage of schools in the poorer areas of the larger cities.

The problem facing schools has been compounded by two far-reaching changes made during the 1970s. The division of schools into primary and secondary was replaced by a three cycle system, while education was made free and compulsory for all students up to the end of the eighth grade. The latter change has involved the nationalisation of all private primary schools which had proliferated in Tehran during the 1960s. Certain exceptions were made. Those foreign schools, mainly established by the staff of foreign embassies but also educating Iranian students, were allowed to continue. It is thought that about 15,000 students are involved. The largest of these schools is the American, closely followed by the Raizi (French) school with 2,500 pupils. The British School is at Qolhak. Another exception are those Iranian schools which have the ministry's permission to follow the curriculum of certain foreign countries, the best established of these being the Jeanne d'Arc School in Tehran, to which the daughters of the more established Tehran families are sent.

Under the reorganisation scheme, primary education has been replaced by the first cycle of general education and covers the first five grades, or years, of a pupil's education. During this cycle there is an emphasis on basic skills resembling the earlier primary schools. The second cycle, starting at the age of eleven, has two separate strands: a simple two-year vocation training course and a three-year educational guidance course. The shorter course is intended for those of limited ability who will probably become manual workers, while the three-year course is designed to assess the student's specialised potential, at the same time continuing his, or her, general education. The third cycle has three alternatives: a four-grade course leading to technical college with a curriculum specifically directed towards this objective; a two-grade course, again technically orientated, designed for those who will become skilled craftsmen; and a four-grade academic course leading on to a university education.

The system is in keeping with the other aspects of Iran's planned development which hopes to be able to estimate future demand in various sectors of the economy. A general education giving basic literacy and numeracy will be provided for all, even the unskilled worker who can be expected to leave school during the second cycle. Various levels of technicians will be provided, with some students starting work after two years' technical studies in the third cycle, while others would go on to technical colleges upon completing this cycle. Additionally, there will also be university-trained scientists, as well as other graduates.

It is a sophisticated system, calling for the most careful structuring of courses, high-quality teachers for the counselling cycles and the most careful monitoring of results. That the system is not working as well as expected is now becoming apparent with the criticisms that are being made. At a recent Ramsar conference, many parents, teachers and students expressed worries about the selection procedure for transfer to second and third cycles—a worry well understood in the UK. 'Even Principals of long experience', the Conference was told, 'are confused and find it difficult to cope with the new system.' The skills being taught in the vocation courses, it was said, are probably irrelevant to the jobs which the pupils will be taking in the future and they will not have sufficient general skills to enable them to be adaptable. The teaching profession 'lashed out at the lack of stability in high school education which, they said, was mainly due to improper planning and repeated changes in laws and regulations concerning high school programmes and students'. A hard-pressed education administrator commented, 'You cannot expect an antiquated system of administration . . . to be capable of handling such large numbers of students and teachers, and to deliver quality education. A thorough overhaul is needed.' Surely he is right.

Now that education is free for the first eight cycles and students may get grants for the last four if they agree to work in Iran for the same number of years afterwards, an intriguing problem has arisen in Tehran. The better known ex-private schools of north Tehran have suddenly found themselves heavily oversubscribed, as pupils from the 'educationally deprived' areas in the south of the city attempt to move up the hill. They have been accused, dare it be said, of taking only those pupils with a high intelligence rating. But some commentators are now suggesting that it may even be necessary that a few schools should be encouraged to maintain academically higher and tougher standards and should cater for students 'whose ambitions and talents are indeed superior'. It would seem that Iran and England have several problems in common, but the Iranian solution will be very different from that in England.

The Shah has become increasingly concerned at the number of families who are sending their children to school in Europe (mainly the UK) and America. At such schools they gain the necessary 'A' levels and other qualifications to attend Western universities. That they should attend Western universities is accepted but the Government is fearful, for the same reason given by Dr Jourdan, about children leaving home at the age of ten or eleven to attend English preparatory and public schools. For some while it has been known that the Shah would favour the establishment within Iran of boarding schools that would closely reflect in tradition, curriculum and ethos British public schools. At such schools the qualifications gained would enable Iranian students to move directly to Western universities at eighteen. A veritable playing-fields of Eton situation in fact— but perhaps on the shores of the Caspian. In the legislation nationalising private schools passed in the summer of 1974, the Shah allowed for the possibility of such schools and said that '(the Government) would not be concerned with the level of fees charged at these schools, but these institutions would cater for only a minority of the population'.

In the spring of 1976 an Imperial Education Council was established, so bringing together a number of earlier education planning groups under the chairmanship of the Shah. It was a recognition of the need for a more balanced appraisal of all aspects of education. During the 1960s, university education had been looked on most favourably and a Ministry for Science and Higher Education was formed in 1967 to develop its role. The added prestige that went with this did not help, it seems, the work of the Ministry of Education. When the Ministry of Science and Higher Education was formed, there were seven universities with a total of 36,000 students. Nine years later, four more universities had been formed, a further eleven were in the process of being designed or built and the student numbers in these and 150 other higher education institutions had increased to 135,000.

Tehran University, with 20,000 students, reflects the multi-discipline of Western universities. Annually, it produces large numbers of graduates in the humanities and social sciences whose future careers would be the richer, and their contribution towards the economy would be the greater, if they had trained in more specific skills. Pahlavi University in Shiraz, with only 4,000 students, has been singularly successful in its science and medical faculties—so successful, in fact, that 80 to 90 per cent of the medical students emigrate to the US upon qualifying. Pahlavi's Chancellor, Dr Fehrang Mehr, said, 'We asked ourselves whether we were justified in devoting all our resources to training a rather small number of highly qualified physicians of recognisable international calibre who were, for that very reason, likely to be lost to our country'. Pahlavi has now established a Department of Community Medicine to train medical personnel at an intermediate level to work alongside fully-qualified doctors in rural areas. 'This particular dimension of relevance', said the Chancellor, 'will take us beyond manpower statistics and defined programme needs. It will attempt to keep us spiritually sane and fit in experimenting with programmes essential to Iran.'

This probably sets the note for further university expansion. When building started on the Bou Ali University in Hamedan, the Empress spoke of its having a special task in the training of experts in rural development programmes. It is generally being accepted that the other new universities will become areas for specialist studies and will not offer the same range of subjects as previously. As Iran struggles to solve its manpower shortages, the length of degree courses, generally four years, is coming under increasing criticism. Iranian society requires, so the arguments go, larger numbers of middle-level technicians for whom a two-year diploma would be satisfactory, if not desirable.

8

How They Get Around

THE deserts and mountains of Iran have presented great challenges to the movement of peoples and goods from the earliest times. No natural routeways follow rivers to the interior and only in the narrow defiles of the mountain passes are routes closely defined by nature. Until recently most Iranians have never left their native villages unless, as nomads, their entire lives have been spent on the annual migration routes. Both villager and nomad have been self-sufficient, requiring nothing and taking only little, if offered, from the outside world. Only the tenets of the Islamic faith have succeeded in moving so many Iranians away from their homes for one long journey in a lifetime by the requirement of pilgrimage. This isolation is, of course, rapidly breaking down but there still remain villages unapproachable by road and people apprehensive of what lies beyond the horizon.

For the traveller, a stout constitution has always been a first essential. Not for nothing did the fiction of magic carpets develop in the minds of men spending days and weeks in the saddle on the back of an earthbound camel! The old routeways that linked city to city and traversed the Iranian plateau as part of a greater network linking Orient to Occident, were but vaguely defined. Along these travelled the Three Wise Men, Marco Polo, warriors, missionaries and numerous traders in silks. Only in the night stopping places, the *caravanserais*, were there fixed points. *Caravanserai*, best described as fortified motels of the desert in an age before cars displaced camels and petrol replaced fodder crops, were built a day's journey apart by

I

enterprising *khans* or commercial companies. When the Empire was strong, the *caravanserais* became official staging posts for government officials and troops protected travellers from bandits; at other times travel became the more dangerous and trade lapsed accordingly.

In 1909, oil men working at Masjid-i-Sulaiman found it preferable to travel to Tehran by boat from the Gulf to Batum on the Russian Black Sea coast, via Suez and Istanbul, thence by train to Baku, ship to Enzeli (Bandar Pahlavi) and onwards by land to Tehran. A diarist at the time wrote of this last part of the journey: 'It is possible, by going right through, to reach Tehran in 50 hours. Then it is best to shut oneself up in a closed carriage and cultivate, if possible, an utter indifference to languor and pain.'

Reza Shah realised the paramount need of improving his internal communications. He devised a system which, at least in theory, sought to integrate railways with roads and trackways. Initially this was to enable him to extend his political control, but it soon became the way by which economic change became possible. Nothing which was incapable of being carried on the back of a camel moved in Iran until Reza Shah's railways started to function in the 1930s. International trade placed only limited demands on the ports of the Caspian and the Gulf; after oil, which was exported through the terminal facilities at Abadan controlled by the British, berries and carpets were the major exports as late as 1940 and these were manhandled from wharf to ship. The demand on the ports, particularly those on the Gulf, and on the road connections with Turkey and to a lesser extent with Pakistan, made by the expansion in the economy has been immense. In 1975, 13 million tons of goods were unloaded at the Gulf ports and so great was the congestion that it was stated that some ships were waiting for 250 days before being able to unload. The entire communication network—road, rail, air and coastal shipping—is now being developed to perform a service and carry a load totally undreamt of a few short years ago.

More than three-quarters of the goods transported are carried by road and it is by road that most people travel. Around each village and town there are tracks and paths, often of great age, that have served local needs for centuries. Rural Iran never really knew the age of the horse-drawn cart, as did Europe or America and it has been the task of the Pahlavis to take the country direct from the pedestrian/camel age to that of the motor car and heavy lorry. With the few exceptions of the toll roads operated by Russians with postchaises, animal tracks have been turned directly into motor roads. When Reza Shah abdicated, it was thought that there were 35,000km of road, but only 8,000 of these were even roughly metalled and the majority were impassable for part of the year. The first roads to be created out of the old trade routes were those linking Tehran to Khorasan, to Qum, Isfahan and the south, to Hamedan, Kermanshah and on to Baghdad, to Tabriz and subsequently to Europe via Turkey, and to Rasht and the ports on the Caspian. By 1975 there were 12,500km of asphalted road, while projections are for all weather-trunk roads to be increased to 20,000km by the end of the Sixth Plan and for 15,500km of asphalted feeder roads to be completed by the same time.

Iranian roads traverse a variety of country, each producing different challenges to the civil engineer and to the driver. Easiest to build are those in the deserts where culverts are first built over the seasonal stream channels and then heavy earth-moving equipment simply pushes and shovels sand and gravel from either side to make a low embankment linking the culverts. The surface is then levelled and treated prior to being asphalted. Progress on such road building is rapid. Not so in the mountains. The skills needed here are equal to, if not exceeding, those in the Alps or the Rockies. The newest roads are a positive triumph of road building skills where new techniques are enabling roads to be built in a fraction of the time required earlier. They may not conform to the high safety requirements of Switzerland but, despite the dangers of loose surfaces and unprotected edges above precipices, they have brought great advantages to the areas they serve. Climatic factors make road maintenance expensive: in the Caspian lowlands heavy rains often sweep away bridges and undermine embankments, in the mountains landslides are all too frequent, particularly in winter but not unheard of at other times of the year; flash floods can destroy culverts even in desert areas; while the extreme heat in so much of Iran can turn asphalt, however it is treated, into toffee.

There are many driving hazards. On unsurfaced roads, by far the greatest number, each vehicle throws up a dust cloud whose size is proportional to that of the vehicle and its speed. Overtaking is hazardous as the driver approaches and enters the dust cloud in front, furiously blowing his horn and flashing his lights to attract the other driver's attention. Not until the tail lights of the front vehicle can be seen will the overtaking driver pull out and hope to get a view of the road in front of him; if an oncoming vehicle is close it is often difficult for the driver to get back out of its way. The noise, the dust, the reverberation of the vehicle on the rough road and the sense of excitement and moments of terror, make overtaking a national sport—of which the foreigner will soon tire! Boredom is another problem, particularly on the straight desert roads which apparently travel on throughout eternity and where the heat and the glare induce mirages. Drivers approaching each other flash all of their myriad lights and sound all of their many-toned horns to ensure that the other driver is awake and aware of the need to share the road. Sometimes they are not and the most hideous head-on accidents occur, frequently hundreds of kilometres away from hospitals. Virtually no roads are fenced. Herds of sheep and goats are always a menace, so too are cattle on the Caspian roads while camels stray without fear on the most remote of desert routes. In the mountains it is the fear of oncoming traffic driven with a reckless disregard for any other person which is the greatest hazard as such vehicles career around the corners sometimes pushing others over the edge of the precipice. Distances between destinations are great and drivers will force themselves to drive for too many hours at too high speeds.

Iranian driving is in a class of its own. 'You British drive with a sense of discipline,' the author's driver once said. 'We

Iranians have a sense of style.' No one can doubt the latter statement, but they may find it hard to accept. Driving in Tehran, with all its associated traffic problems, is downright dangerous. Iranians, so often charming, sympathetic, kind and humane, become positive Jehu's behind the wheel—more pejorative descriptions are common. Accidents are frequent: 'very few Tehran cars are unscathed by minor scratches while the remnants of hideous head-on collisions and vehicles, sometimes buses, neatly sliced in two as they have tried to overtake one another, are grim reminders of the rigours of driving outside the cities.'

The first freeway built in Iran was that linking Tehran to Karaj, with work having been started in the mid-1970s to extend this to Qazvin and Takestan. A total of over 1,700km of freeway are expected to be in operation by 1983 which will, amongst other things, link Tehran to Isfahan and Tehran to Ahvaz and onwards to Bandar Shahpur, both by way of Qum. Short lengths of urban freeways are being provided in Tehran and Isfahan. Great efforts are being made to fully integrate the southern ports of Khorramshahr, Bandar Shahpur, Bushehr and Bandar Abbas into the national network. This will involve much road construction in the south-east where the links between Yazd and Kerman are being improved and a vastly expanded road network is being designed to focus on the latter. Some improvements are being made to the north–south route between Sistan and Khorasan and a totally new road is planned to link Tehran to Mashad.

During the nineteenth century, many railway projects were suggested, frequently by the British, to link India to Europe, and by the Russians, to link the Gulf to the Caspian, but only a few scattered miles had been built before Reza Shah's project to build the Trans-Iranian Railway. This was started in 1927 and finished in 1939. It linked Bandar Shah on the Caspian to Bandar Shahpur on the Gulf. It was 860 miles in length and financed entirely by internal taxes rather than international loans. 4,100 bridges were built and 224 tunnels with an aggregate length of 54 miles were dug. Its construction was, at the time, a positive triumph over difficulties of terrain, design, materials and manpower problems. In the late 1950s the railway network was extended to Mashad in the east and Tabriz in the west and linked through to the Russian system via Jolfa. In 1972, the CENTO-sponsored rail link with Europe through Turkey was open (CENTO stands for the Central European Treaty Organisation). Currently there are 4,500km of railway lines with a further 10,000 either in the course of construction or planned. The existing lines are being modernised to provide for an electrified service along the Tabriz–Tehran–Mashad axial route where turbo-trains operating at speeds of up to 250km are projected. The original line linking Bandar Shahpur to Tehran is being virtually rebuilt: gradients are being reduced, double tracking introduced and the entire route electrified. In keeping with its policy of unimpeded expansion of the Gulf ports the Government has placed no credit restrictions on this project nor on the other project linking Bandar Abbas with Sirjan and the Yazd-Kerman line and the final link between Zarand and Kerman. A second, completely separate route, is to duplicate the Tabriz–Qazvin–Tehran–Ahvaz–Bandar Shahpur line. Planning has started on projects to link Bandar Abbas to the national network via Baft and Kerman, and Bushehr with a line through Shiraz to Isfahan. Other projects look to a Gulf coast route linking all the ports and a Mashad to Chahbahar route along Iran's eastern border.

Enzeli, the present Bandar Pahlavi, was for a long while the major Iranian port and through here passed most of the European trade bound for the Russian port of Baku. The British developed Abadan and Reza Shah singled out Bandar Shahpur as the main general purpose cargo port for the Gulf. In the early 1940s the combined daily capacity of Bandar Shahpur and Khorramshahr was about 4,000 tons a day. Improvements since then have been continuous, but totally insufficient to deal with the demands that were suddenly placed on them from 1974 onwards. Not only have the ports been unable to deal with the large number of boats waiting to unload but they have been unable to clear the cargo once it has been unloaded. The problems reached epic proportions in 1975 when it was recorded that ships were waiting as much as five months at Khorramshah and three months at Bandar Shahpur before being able to unload. On land, more than a million tons of goods were stuck in the cargo areas at Khorramshah waiting to be moved; similar conditions prevailed at the other ports. Waiting times at Bushehr and Bandar Abbas have not been as great, but the clearance of cargo inland has produced even greater problems for these ports which have to rely entirely on road transport. Much cargo perished before it could be properly stored. As great as was the tonnage handled in 1975, there was a further 20 per cent increase in 1976. Tremendous efforts were made during 1976 to improve the port-handling facilities and various short and long-term solutions were found. Unloading capacity, which had been little more than 6,000 tons a day in early 1975, rose to 17,000 tons by late 1976 and the waiting time for ships dropped accordingly. The problem of insufficient lorries and drivers to move the goods inland was eventually solved by the purchase of large numbers of heavy trucks and trailers from abroad (which, in turn, were stuck on board ships waiting to be unloaded) and the recruitment of foreign drivers.

In an effort to beat the port jams more and more trade entered Iran by road. Manchester Liners introduced a new sea/land route via the Mediterranean port of Iskenderum in July 1975, but this was only one of many factors that helped to jam the customs post at Bazargum where over 5,000 juggernauts were waiting clearance by November. The wear and tear on Turkish roads became considerable and has led to much friction between the Turkish and Iranian Governments. By the end of 1975, 9 per cent of all imports were passing through this border post by lorry. Goods from India even began to enter Iran by road to beat the port jam.

Proposals have been made to increase the handling capacity of the ports to a total of 29 million tons a year which, when implemented, should give spare capacity for several years. Bandar Shahpur is expected to handle just over half of this and the new port to be built to the west of Bandar Abbas is to be designed for a capacity of 10 million tons per annum. Bushehr will have a capacity of a million tons, Khorramshahr will continue at its present level and the new port of Chahbahar in the extreme south-east will have some cargo-handling capacity. The handling capacity of Caspian ports of Bandar Pahlavi and Nowshahr will be increased to just under a million tons. The need to improve the ports and all levels of internal communication is so great and so fundamental to the development of the other areas of the economy that the Government made this the prime area for investment in the Revised Plan.

Nearly all travellers now arrive in Iran at Tehran's Mehrabad Airport. This was built in 1958 and became the base of Iran's national airline, Iran Air, when it was formed in 1962. The increase in traffic has been prodigious. The mid-1960s saw some fifty aircraft a day and $\frac{1}{4}$ million passengers a year while, ten years later, it was 250 aircraft and 2·5 million passengers with a real possibility that there could be 5 million passengers by 1978. The airport has been extended many times and plans were announced in early 1970 for a new international airport to be built to the south of the city. Iran Air and many other airlines give good and frequent services to many countries. Iran Air, with a fleet containing 747s, 747SPs and with a firm commitment to add three Concordes has established a good international reputation. Internal services are being expanded all the time and now serve twenty cities and more airfields are being developed.

A small number of travellers, mainly tourists and students, enter Iran by rail through Turkey or by rail and boat from Russia and the Caspian to Bandar Pahlavi. Some reach Iran by bus from Europe through Bazargum or by car from Turkey, Afghanistan or Pakistan. Within Iran, the proportion of travellers to modes of transport is probably the same as it is for goods: 80 per cent by road, 16 per cent by rail and the remaining 4 per cent mainly by air—but the day of the camel has not yet passed and some people and goods still travel as they have done for millennia.

Most people travelling by road rely on buses: bus services

throughout the country are extremely well organised, relatively cheap, frequently maintain faster times than cars and, as many Iranians will admit, if you are going to have a crash you are better off in a bus than in a car! Be that as it may, buses are to be recommended for all those travelling great distances in areas where trains do not run and where the air service is not appropriate. A journey from Tehran to Shiraz, a distance of some 900km, will cost about R300 (£2) for a journey equivalent to that between London and Inverness or New York and Detroit. Service is good, with drinks served while travelling, and well planned stops at suitable eating houses— sometimes situated in old *caravanserais*. Railway services are steadily improving and new rolling stock is being purchased. There are no less than eight grades of class from which to choose when buying a ticket! Costs are higher than for a comparable bus journey but Mashad can be reached from Tehran (900km) for fares ranging between R350 and R1025. No alcohol is served on this pilgrimage line. The same journey can be made by Iran Air for R3,800 first class or R3,000 second class.

No one method of travel within Iran commends itself beyond all others. The traveller wishing to experience the country to the full is recommended to try them all, from the national airline to the camel, the donkey—or his own climbing boots in the mountains!

9

How They Amuse Themselves

'PARADISE' is a Persian word. To a Persian it does not have connotations of an other-worldly heaven: it is far more immediate and more attainable but, none the less, beautiful and desirable. 'Paradise' means a walled garden; a place of calm, of cool and soft green colours with the sound of running water in a ditch; a place in which to relax after the heat, dryness and the stark monotony of the desert. Practical it may well be, but it was paradise not only to the camelteers and the caravans lumbering out of the desert in years gone by, it also remains singularly attractive to urban Iranians of the twentieth century. 'We have a garden outside the city, it is very beautiful,' a sophisticated Tehrani will say. 'You must come with us on Friday and we will have a picnic.' Any vision of an English-style country garden with a mass of roses, pansies, dahlias and wallflowers all backed by an Ann Hathaway-type cottage set against a Persian blue sky will be rudely shattered when your host ushers you through the gate in the mud-brick wall that surrounds his garden. Here is greenness and shade, the smell of sweet-scented jasmine, coolness and probably the sound of running water—but, oh, what disorder! The grass is probably rank, boughs of the trees broken and the roses, if they exist at all, are the climbing kind covering some fallen tree. If the Iranian does not romanticise about the design of his garden he surely romanticises about its use! Beautiful rugs are produced and, with great thought to the pattern of the shade, the breeze, the scents from the plants and the nearness to the water, placed for the guest to sit upon. The magic of the scene becomes increasingly apparent. Fruit is passed around;

great peaches of a size unobtainable in the West, apricots, apples and large, succulent pears. Polite little fruit knives and plates reminiscent of an earlier European tradition are passed around. Tea is produced from a sizzling samovar and the ladies, or servants, depending on the class and income of your host, prepare the first of many dishes that will comprise the meal and occupy most of the afternoon. So far the scene is timeless and paradise—be it Eastern or Western in concept—may well seem a little closer. Then it is suddenly shattered. Your host, with great pride, produces the latest and most expensive of Japanese transistor radios and, for your benefit, tunes in to some popular radio station for a continuous programme of Western popular music played at maximum volume!

Here within the Persian paradise, if the analogy may be pushed so far, is the conflict of modern Iran. Iran, sitting astride so many trade routes has seen many cultures over the centuries and been ruled by many conquerors. But Iranian history shows that invariably the conquerors have themselves been Iranian-ised and the culture of the land has continued the richer by the incorporation of new ideas. But the present conflict between Eastern and Western thought, between Eastern mysticism with its acceptance of the will and overriding purposes of Allah, and Western materialism with the Christian (perhaps more specifically Protestant) ethic of self-help and free will, can hardly result in a compromise. Perhaps the early Persians were able to survive the invasion of Genghis Khan, of Tamerlane and even Alexander, with less threat to their identity than can modern Iran resist the influence of Western culture and its all-pervading influence through the medium of transistor radio.

The very title of this chapter is essentially a result of a Western concept. In writing about the subject, it is necessary to realise the limitations that it places on the understanding of a people. The Western concept of amusement, and more precisely how a people 'organise' its amusement, does not provide a satisfactory framework to describe this aspect of Iranian life. To the tribesman constantly migrating through the Zagros Mountains, his amusement is part of his way of life, conditioned by nature and the demands of survival. To the nomadic desert dwellers or inhabitants of small desert towns, life is tough and the need for survival paramount. To the small merchant in the bazaar, the peasant farmer and the fisherman of the Caspian, organised amusement has, in times past, played but an insignificant part in his life. For the urban Iranian, however, life has changed dramatically. The cities boast their cinemas, parks and a wide range of clubs and restaurants while the Government is doing much to stimulate organised games and youth activities. As Iran becomes more urbanised, so the concept of organised amusement must, inevitably, spread.

Iran at present, perhaps more so than at any time in its history is a land of contrast. Nowhere is this contrast more apparent than in the way people amuse themselves when the cares of survival, in nomadic tent or high rise office block, can be forgotten. It leads to situations of pure farce. On the shores of the Karaj reservoir is an extremely modern hotel doubling as a yacht club. To many Iranians it is the ultimate status symbol of the good life: deep carpets, air-conditioning, chrome fittings all engender an atmosphere that is blandly international. Cabaret, featuring European songs and singers, is provided but of a quality that hardly merits the extremely high prices charged. A few kilometres away, a group of workmen pause whilst working on a bridge repair; being Kurds and country people as yet unaffected by the cultural hang-ups they dance one imagines for sheer enjoyment, a dance of great energy and beauty that would do credit to a cabaret anywhere. This free and unsolicited show is largely ignored by the cars that speed by or the dancers dismissed as being 'ignorant people' by the drivers who minutes later pull up for the night at the lakeside hotel and think nothing of paying twenty-four dollars for a bottle of whisky.

So great is the contrast in lifestyles that it can be understood only by looking at both traditional and progressive attitudes towards the use of free time and the amusements that have developed.

TRADITIONAL

Iranians are, and always have been, an hospitable people. It is perhaps in their forms of hospitality that they have, from earliest times, amused themselves. In a country where travel has always been arduous, frequently hazardous, hospitality— a first duty imposed by the Koran—is an essential to civilised living. While all responsible travellers plan and have planned their itineraries from *caravanserai* to *caravanserai* or tent site to tent site, accidents inevitably occur, making the need to depend on one's neighbours great.

At its most frequent and simplest level is the drinking of tea. Suburban England cannot compare to this art as practised by the Iranians! In the corners of a field, in a farmer's home, in the bazaar, a government office or even in the street, a samovar is always available. Glasses of strong dark tea are drunk by all and sundry and offered, it would seem, regardless of cost. The casual visitor to a home or office will frequently be regaled with fruit as well. The best of Iranian cooking is to be found in the home, not in inns or eating houses. Meals are for enjoyment; Iranians don't just eat to live. A meal is never a hurried affair but something to be lingered over, talked through and to encourage relaxation.

The visitor who can get away from urban Iran and be entertained by a farmer or the village *kadkhodah* is indeed fortunate. To sit cross-legged in the cool of a mud-brick village house on valuable carpets piled two or three thick, with a fan in one's hand to keep away the flies is a memorable experience. After the inevitable preliminaries of tea and fruit come plates of cheese, fried eggs, omelettes, rice, goulash, butter, bread and sweetcakes. Invariably, the number of guests builds up during the meal and the room becomes crowded with relations, neighbours, maybe the local gendarme, the Literacy Corps worker and endless numbers of children. In an atmosphere of friendly banter the host distributes more and more hospitality.

Discussion, after some desultory questioning of the visitor about the need for irrigation in his home country or the price of rice, potatoes or sunflower seed in England, inevitably comes back to the needs of the village and the almost childlike naivety expressed in the power of Government to supply every facility within the next one, or at least two, years.

Almost gone now from the Iranian countryside are the remnants of the more aristocratic existence associated with the grandees of the *Qajar* dynasty and the big landowners prior to the White Revolution. In homes which were (and still are in a few isolated instances) a delightful, if curious, mixture of mud-brick structure, housing priceless treasures of Iranian and Parisian furnishings, was to be found a level of hospitality from which grew the popular fables of the East. Guests were welcomed in numbers, while their drivers and other entourage were accommodated in the servants' quarters. As one course of food was replaced by the next, the remains of the former were passed outside to be consumed by the retainers. The number of courses could be almost limitless. Although strong drink is specifically banned by the Koran, good local wines have for centuries been associated with small, private vineyards in the foothills of the Elburz, around Isfahan and in the further south near Shiraz and Kerman. At such feasts these wines would flow. So too in later years, does whisky, in deference to the Western palate.

Disappearing also are the tribes and a way of life that was rich in customs and traditions in which events, such as the wedding of a *khan*'s daughter, were celebrated with great feasts. The glamour that has now almost gone strikes an increasing nostalgia amongst Iranians. The riches of the Bakhtiari and the Quashquai and the feasts which they gave for their tribes to mark such festivities lasting days on end, are something which the modern traveller will have to read about rather than experience.

Like all country and small town dwellers the world over, Iranians get great enjoyment from their everyday lives. Be it the purchase of a sheep or tomatoes or a beautiful Persian rug, the transaction is full of dramatic potential—it is not to be hurried but enjoyed. The bazaar is as much an intrinsic part of the Iranian economy as the haggling over prices is an intrinsic part of their lifestyle. To the Westerner in a hurry it is frustrating to a degree, but to the shopkeeper it is a way of showing that he is servant of none and will do trade on his terms—and his alone. The negotiated price for tomatoes is, by its nature, rapidly concluded but not so the sale of carpets. No one knows how many carpets are made annually in Iran, nor, if carpet-making were to cease, how the people so released from their manufacture would spend their newly acquired free time. More than anything else in rural Iran, wealth and status have been measured in terms of these beautiful hand-knitted rugs which serve, in addition to investments, as floor coverings, beds, chairs and table coverings. Their purchase is a lengthy affair; indeed, the carpet section of any bazaar is the least frantic part of the whole complex. Carpets are inspected at length, with detailed questions of their antecedents, design, colours, style, quality . . . and their value is discussed in great depth over innumerable glasses of tea before a single offer is placed. It is a national pastime not chronicled in any year book nor tabulated like a football competition but nevertheless very real, very enjoyable and very Iranian.

Perhaps it is amongst the farming community that the idea of working for enjoyment rather than working to obtain a living with sufficient money left over for amusement, is most finely developed. Statistics, for what they are worth, show that there are twenty-five million sheep and thirteen million goats in Iran. Most of them are to be found on the open hill sides tended by countless shepherds and shepherd boys. Some of these men and boys are as skilled with a sling as was David, nimble and fleet of foot, marksmen of no mean merit, shooting leopard, wolf and bear, tellers of tales and singers of songs in a tradition older than man's written history. Organised amusement they do not have, but, increasingly, their job is being made the more difficult by urban Iranians entering the same hills with rifles to shoot the same leopard, wolf and bear in the name of sport and for their amusement.

The arable farmers, too, have their moments of sheer enjoyment. The West has largely forgotten the significance of the harvest moon—not so the grain farmers of Iran. The fields have to be kept irrigated during the growing season and the ripe crop must be harvested by hand. Then it is taken to the threshing-floors where the oxen tread it patiently underfoot for days prior to the long hours of winnowing, still done by hand with large wooden forks when there is a strong wind to carry away the chaff. By the time of the harvest moon this activity has reached its peak and the carrying has already begun. The full moon is celebrated by all the villagers with dancing and feasting in the fields in a tradition pre-dating the religious celebrations of Islam, Christianity and, maybe, even Zoroaster.

Of Islamic origin are the pilgrimages to sacred places. For most Iranians, until quite recently, these would be the only journey they would ever make away from their native town or village. While essentially a religious duty, a pilgrimage has always given an opportunity for excitement, a break from routine, a personal challenge—all crowned with the thrill of the achievement of reaching the site of pilgrimage. Within Iran itself, Mashad, the burial place of Reza the 8th Iman, is the chief centre of pilgrimage, closely followed by Qum at the shrine of Fatima, sister of the 8th Iman. To the Iranian Shia Moslems, a number of sacred sites in Iraq also attract pilgrimage. Chief site of pilgrimage is, of course, Mecca.

MODERN

If the amusements of traditional Iran are but extensions of people's work so that enjoyment is essentially an aspect of everyday activity, the more Western concept of amusement as a separate activity, pursued with energy and enthusiasm in the expectation that it will yield enjoyment, is well developed amongst urban dwellers, certainly the more well-to-do. To the office worker of Tehran, the harvest moon, pilgrimage, tribal weddings and essential hunting trips are as far removed from his experience as are the backwoods for the American or crofting for the Scot. Of immediate significance is the morning traffic jam, the price of an apartment, the numbers of days' holiday, the doctor's fees. There is no reason to suppose that the lot of the office worker, be it of cabinet minister or secretary, is any better or worse in Tehran than that of his or her colleague in Washington, London or Paris. Enjoyment they may well find in their work but, when that is over, what next? It is a problem that modern Iran is still grappling with, but so, too, is the West if the number of seminars on 'The problem of Leisure' are any guide.

The conflict between Eastern and Western thought ex-emplified by the modern transistor radio in the traditional garden is harsher and more compelling when experienced in the cities. Not only is Western materialism the more obvious, deafening and blinding, but the people are terrifyingly ill-prepared to cope with the problems of selection that such a culture imposes. The cities of Iran, Tehran in particular, have grown very rapidly so that millions of their inhabitants are first generation urban stock. The transition for a peasant farmer from a mountain village to the poorer parts of south Tehran will be difficult and depressing, whilst the transition for a post high school youngster from the provinces to Tehran University or a government post will subject him to considerable culture shock.

Organised amusements in Iranian cities are still in their infancy; to the entrepreneur looking for an opening and with sufficient capital to invest, the chances of making a fortune must rate very high. The urban Iranian is looking for substitutes for those activities which have given his ancestors enjoyment in the past; if he can find these directly he will take them, but if he can't he will take whatever alternative other cultures can offer him. Hospitality on the traditional scale is difficult to provide in a Tehran apartment block, the home of some of the richest and most successful government officials and professional people. So there have grown up large numbers of highly successful eating houses, restaurants and hotels specialising in Iranian,

K

European and specialities of other nationalities. The food is lavish, the cooking varies from moderate to very good, the surroundings opulent and the service—if the prospect of a good tip is imminent—obsequious. To these gourmet delights will go not courting couples or business acquaintances but whole family parties and families entertaining families. What was the reserve of the home has been taken out to the realms of the speculative caterer and a price put on hospitality— not infrequently leading to heated disputes between the senior males when the bill is produced as to who is to pay the bill, which may easily pass the £100 mark for only a moderate- sized dinner party. A few years ago a writer could confidently predict that the best food would be found at the Park or Mar Mar hotels or the French Club. Now one would not be so rash. Fashions change and fortunes are made and lost. The smaller restaurants rise with meteoric speed to fame, and die again. Once it was Leoni's (with a speciality in Russian food) then Chez Michel and, at the other extreme, Ray's Pizza House Nos 1 and 2, the Sorrento, Chattanoga or the Hatam Chicken Kebab. Perhaps some of the most bristling of trade is to be found in the outdoor restaurants of the Royal Tehran Hilton and the most exclusive on the top floor of the Intercontinental.

In its search for amusement, urban Iran moves as frantically as it does in so many other spheres. Hotels are used like clubs but still charge as hotels. The old well established European clubs still survive but their prestige is not as high as it might be because they don't charge exorbitant prices, their food is positively ordinary and their atmosphere informal. The dilet- tantism of the educated European middle classes is not under- stood by the rising Iranian executive even though he may still inherit from older colleagues a sneaking fear that perhaps they have something which he has missed out on completely. With nostalgia, senior government officials or civil servants may re- call how they once joined a friend on the staff of the British Embassy for a weekend at the Embassy's summer camp in the Lar Valley where the facilities, amongst scenery of great beauty, were somewhat basic and reminiscent of scouting and public-school traditions. They would like to re-create the experience, but overdo the expenditure, have electricity in the tents, uncomfortable boots, new and highly expensive fishing lines—and end up disappointed and with an underlying fear that their friends will see in this a sign that financially they have not got as much money as they would like. Iranian academics find it incomprehensible that British professors visiting Tehran are more prepared to sleep on the roof of the British Institute for Persian Studies and drink tea in a comfortable if cluttered library than they are to stay in a modern hotel.

Yet the attitude suggested by the telling of these anecdotes is essentially unfair. Europe and America have had time to come to terms with materialism—not so Iran. Some Europeans simply prefer things that don't cost money; some have no money and try to exist off other people. Iran has seen, recently, too many of the latter as the hippy trail crossed the country to Katmandu leaving behind it disgust in the eyes of many Iranians for the petty thefts, sexual assault and the use of hard drugs.

Modern Iran does little reading for recreation, though it studies extremely hard at the universities, particularly in maths and sciences. In Tehran it is difficult to find a book shop, though paper and magazine stands also selling cigarettes and chewing gum are to be found on every street. Statistics show that there are only fifty-two bookshops and fifteen libraries in the whole city. Few books are published in Iran and those which come from abroad, while available in some shops, are expensive They range from the specialised scientific, through the classics, to the more lurid of modern fiction. Pirate editions of books published abroad are also to be found on the bookshelves. Some people measure the cultural life of a city by its bookshops; by this criterion Iranian cities show up badly, but it is essentially a Western attitude which should not be applied too rigorously. It will take more years than the optimists expect for a reading habit to develop amongst the people and, when it does, it will be interesting to see what it demands. Certainly, the confusion now presiding in bookshops which can put *The Adventures of Tin-Tin*, a Persian grammar, a work on hydrology and a James Bond novel alongside will not survive. Perhaps a sign of the times is the fact that recently the best seller, in Farsi, was *How to Maintain Your Motor Car*—not that the number of books printed is very great, amounting in total to one book a year for every ten literate Iranians.

If libraries and bookshops are few and far between even scarcer are toy shops and hobby suppliers, particularly of the indoor variety. If Froebel and many other child psychologists are to be believed, toys are essential to a child's early development, not to mention the satisfaction of the parents indulging their own fantasies with dolls and train sets! The official statistics do not record how many toy shops there are, but a guess would put this in single figures. Of course, toys and games can be purchased in other shops, but they tend to be mainly gimmicks and very expensive. Few toys are made in Iran and the imports attract high tariffs.

If books, toys, games and hobbies are in short supply in modern urban Iran, radio, television, hi-fi and other electronic equipment seems to be present on a lavish scale. Twenty-four radio stations cover the country, supplying an estimated 10 million radio sets and give an 80 per cent coverage, while television services can now be received over about half the country. Television sets have increased from 150,000 to more than 2 million in ten years. There are three channels available in Tehran while fourteen other cities have their own independent services. The quality of home-produced programmes varies considerably but, with a growth from twenty-one to over seventy hours of transmission a week in only seven years, this is to be expected. The equipment for both transmission and receiving, is of the most sophisticated kind, being imported from Japan and America. In the Iranian home, TV still holds the same novelty attraction as it did in Western countries a generation or more ago and the ability to 'turn off' has yet to be developed. Also imported from Japan and West Germany is a vast range of record-playing equipment. Much of this is highly sophisticated and very expensive. Records and tapes are mainly imported, and reflect almost entirely the foreign culture of their place of origin.

The Ministry of Culture seeks to encourage Iranian artists—be they musicians, actors, folk singers, directors, composers—anyone, in fact, who can help to create entertainment which is specifically Iranian. With the ever-increasing popularity, and availability, of radio and television the need for this is pressing if the country is not to be swamped by an alien culture.

Tribal life had a rich, if largely unrecorded, musical tradition; drama, frequently in an extemporised form, was once a common feature of both urban and rural Iran; poetry, popular with all classes of Iranians for centuries, has a rich tradition which has fed modern creative thought. During the earlier stages of the Pahlavi era these traditions were ignored as being reactionary but, recently, interest in them has been renewed and they have become a source of inspiration for new work. Iranian culture has, until now, been based on the needs of small groups, those that could be accommodated in one room or in an outdoor arena, probably around a camp fire. There has been a close interplay between performer and spectator, with little reliance on written material. In responding to the needs of the modern theatre, radio or television, the changes that have had to be made are very considerable. The evolution is not as yet complete.

There are only a dozen theatres in Iran and more than half of these are in Tehran. The largest, the Theatre Shahr, seats 700 people. Most of the plays produced are, despite the attempts to produce Iranian material, translations of foreign plays. The choice of such plays has, not infrequently, led the actors into conflict with the authorities. NIRTV (National Iranian Radio and Television) sponsors the theatre and uses its productions on the television networks; it also encourages the film industry so that, currently, some seventy films a year are being made. The Ministry of Culture, however, maintains a strict control over the contents of the films, much to the annoyance of the writers and producers. This is done '. . . to encourage the producers to select subjects of high moral standard . . .' Despite the limitations and frustrations, the standard of production is rising rapidly and several Iranian films have recently received international acclaim.

There is only one opera house in Tehran, the Rudaki, which was opened in 1968. The majority of works performed are by foreign composers but works by Iranian composers are also presented. Iran is now able to sponsor foreign ballet companies and orchestras to perform in Tehran and such events are becoming increasingly frequent. The National Iranian Ballet Company sends its members to train with European companies whilst relying on Russian choreographers for its own productions. The Tehran Symphony Orchestra was formed in the late 1950s; its history has been somewhat stormy with all the artists resigning in 1972 in protest against the appointment of a new conductor. Iranian folk music has become very popular. While it is certainly local in origin, it has similarities with Western popular music which has helped to make it acceptable to the progressive Iranian music enthusiast. Some Iranian folk singers, particularly Gougoush, have large followings and this has stimulated the growth of numerous small folk-music groups throughout the country.

The Shiraz Arts Festival, inaugurated in 1967, has now become an annual event. Intended as a bridge between eastern and western traditions, it has contained material ranging from the excellent to the frankly boring. The Festival is under the patronage of Empress Farah. Situated in Shiraz, and thus away from the full bureaucratic direction of the capital, the event is more spontaneous, more realistic, more human than would be the case if it were intended as a showpiece. In its fringe activities it resembles the Edinburgh Festival.

Plays, concerts and operas are, however, of interest only to a minority. Mass entertainment is provided by the cinema, of which there are now over 500 in 140 towns and cities, Tehran alone having 125. On average, every citizen of Tehran goes to the cinema six times a year and pays R35 on each occasion. The majority of the films are imported, many from the West but a significant number from India and Turkey. If censorship of the film industry is strict, the bill hoardings outside the cinemas are garish in the extreme.

For some 200,000 young Iranians the Boy Scout organisation provides a more active recreation than the cinema. Scouting was established in Iran during the reign of Reza Shah but was abandoned during World War II and not restarted until 1962. Unlike many Western countries, the State finances scouting in Iran and the 10,000 scout masters are paid accordingly. Activities are of a more social, less arduous, nature than in the West. In 1979 the World Scout Jamboree is due to be held in Isfahan. The number of scouts is expected to have reached half a million by 1978 but, even then, will only involve a minority of the country's youth. The large number of unoccupied youths causes the Government great concern; such spare, undirected time can lead, it is stated, to 'political deviation, or the senseless imitation of the so-called "Western industrial civilisation" '. The Red Lion and Sun organisation, Iran's largest charity and roughly comparable to the Red Cross (it is financed out of oil revenues) has opened a number of Youth Palaces in the provinces which provide a wide range of sporting and social activities.

Iran is the home of polo which is thought to have originated in Isfahan, where it was played on the Maidan-e-Shah before the Ali Qapu palace. The stone goal posts still stand at either end of this once magnificent pitch. Another Persian sport, still practised and to be seen in Tehran and elsewhere, is to be found in the Zurkhaneh, or House of Strength. Within this, teams of strong and agile men perform prodigious feats of gymnastics in time to the music and the chanting of their leader. The origin of this is lost in history but it certainly contains elements that are distinctly tribal and certainly religious.

Soccer is the country's most popular sport, and is now played at international level. In 1975, 100,000 Iranians watched Hungary narrowly beat their home team 2–1. In the same year English teams of note, West Ham and Manchester United, played in Iran; Iran beat Iraq; Persepolis 'blasted' Taj for the premier place in the League; while Tabriz Tractors, a 2nd

Division team, bid R1 million for goalkeeper Nasser Hejazi to be transferred from successful Shahbaz. Promotion and relegation between leagues is a hotly disputed issue. It all sounds very English—and it is. Frank O'Farrell of Manchester United was signed up in 1974 as National Coach and plans have been discussed for the Football Association to establish coaching schools in Iran. Newspapers encourage the enthusiasts: 'Taj beaten 2–0 by Persepolis'; 'Taj blast Tabriz'; 'Unbeaten Homa hold Burma'; 'Mighty Taj slam to the top'; 'Iran made it! Now meet Iraq'; 'Khorasan for the title' . . . and so on and so on. As in England, so in Iran, soccer is an excellent game for the masses both as a participator and, increasingly, spectator sport. Soon the league structure will grow to embrace all the country. The building of the Aryamehr Sports Stadium for the seventh Asian Games held in Tehran in September 1974 marked a significant landmark in the development of sport within Iran. Amongst its facilities are a 100,000-seat stadium, a 12,000-seat sports hall and a 4,000-seat swimming pool.

Iran is determined to establish for herself an important place in world sport. Hopes for Olympic successes at both Munich and Montreal were not realised but, undaunted, Iran has offered to host the Olympics of 1984. Through its individual sporting organisations Iran has bid widely to host a number of other events, ranging from the International Chess Olympiad to the World Youth Boxing Championships and the Asian Tennis Tournament—the Aryamehr Tennis Tournament now being the world's fourth richest after Wimbledon, Forest Hills and Paris. While such a policy is obviously based on focusing international attention on Iran, it is proving a much needed tonic for world sport faced with the ever-increasing cost of international competition.

Many sports are played, as elsewhere, purely for recreation. At the Imperial Country Club off Pahlavi Avenue, the Tehrani may play tennis, ride, swim or just eat and drink in pleasant surroundings. The richest families have their own tennis courts and swimming pools. Water sports are being developed wherever possible. Ski-ing is a popular winter sport for Tehranis on the hill slopes above the city, while outside Hamedan, on the slopes of Mt Alwand, a major ski centre is being built. Hunting has always been popular in a country with a wide variety of wild life—red deer, wild goat, boar, Asian brown bear, leopard, wolf and gazelle. For the wealthy Tehrani, the ultimate status symbol is a property on the Caspian shore. In the last twenty years, and more particularly in the past two or three, these have proliferated to such an extent that they are now a serious threat to a once beautiful area. Some of the properties are converted farmsteads, others elaborate architect-designed luxury homes, while too many have been hurriedly erected by speculative builders. The traffic between Tehran and the Caspian is so heavy that the passes of Chalus-Karaj and Amol-Abe Ali are turned into what must be the world's largest one-way system, or giant roundabout, at the weekends.

In its relaxation, as in its work, Iran is a country of contrast. But the contrasts of yesterday are not those of today . . . and those of today are unlikely to be those of tomorrow.

Acknowledgements

THE author would like to extend his sincere thanks to the following:

Ole Sippel of Danish Television and the BBC for permission to quote from broadcasts, *The Times* for granting permission to quote from certain articles and to *Newsweek* for similar approval. The majority of photographs have been provided by the Iran National Tourist Office; the remainder have been taken by the author.

Invaluable help has been given by Anne Brown and Vera Hones, Phillip Boden, Roy Cross and Tony Gelsthorpe, with many suggestions from Dr Iraj Barahman and Dr Khoshnovisian and numerous other Iranian friends. A special word of thanks is due to members of the Manchester Grammar School and Young Explorers' Trust Expeditions for ideas, facts and general stimulation, to Shrah and Trinity College, Dublin, and, in particular, to his wife Anne.

Bibliography

Amirsadeghi, H. *Twentieth Century Iran* (Heinemann, 1977)

Arberry, A. J. *The Legacy of Persia* (Oxford University Press, 1953)

Arfa, A. *Under Five Shahs* (John Murray, 1964)

Armajani, Y. *Iran* (Prentice-Hall Inc, 1972)

Blunt, W. *Isfahan Pearl of Persia* (Elek Books, 1966)

British Admiralty Handbook (Naval Intelligence Division, 1975)

Clarke, J. I. and Fisher, W. B. *Populations of the Middle East and North Africa* (ULP, 1972)

Cronin, V. *The Last Migration* (Rupert Hart-Davis, 1957)

Curzon, The Hon G. C. *Persia and the Persian Question* (Longmans, 1892)

Denman, D. R. *The King's Vista* (Geographical Publications Ltd, 1973)

Fisher, W. B. *The Land of Iran* (Cambridge History of Iran, 1968)

Frye, R. N. *The Heritage of Persia* (Weidenfeld & Nicolson, 1962)

Hone, J. N. *Persia in Revolution* (Maunsel, 1910)

Lambton, A. K. S. *The Persian Land Reform* (Oxford University Press, 1969)

Matheson, S. A. *Persia: An Archaeological Guide* (Faber, 1972)

Nouri, A. H. N. *Iran's Contribution to the World Civilisation* (Tehran, 1971)

Shah, H. I. M. *Mission for My Country* (McGraw Hill, 1961)

Stark, F. *The Valley of the Assassins* (John Murray, 1936)

Stevens, R. *The Land of the Great Sophy* (Methuen, 1962)

Wright, D. *Persia* (Thames & Hudson, 1969)

MAGAZINES AND PERIODICALS

Kayhan International. Tehran (weekly)
Middle East Economic Digest. London (weekly)
The Times Special Reports. London
Newsweek. New York (weekly)
Iran Almanack (Echo) Tehran (yearly)

Plan and Budget Organisation Reports in particular *Iran Fifth Development Plan: Revised* (May 1975) and *Statistical Year Books*

Index

This index is necessarily selective. Most of the historical material has been omitted. So also has reference to the present Shah, whose name appears on most pages. Reference has not been made to the British and the Russians, whose names and the various alternatives for their countries occur with increasing frequency towards the end.